34/-

Essays in Moral Philosophy

Essays in
Moral Philosophy

EDITED BY **A. I. Melden**

University of Washington Press
Seattle 1958

Contents

Introduction

During recent years there has been a remarkable growth of interest in moral philosophy. It would be difficult to determine the extent to which progress has been achieved in the rash of books and journal articles that have seen the light of day during the last decade or so. No doubt much of this published material represents at best interesting but unsuccessful philosophical moves, and some of it clearly exhibits the chronic philosophic vice of discussing in high-level generalities matters that can be handled successfully only when close attention is paid to details. But, even if nothing fundamentally new and enlightening has emerged, excitement has been in the air and the conviction fairly widespread that progress in moral philosophy, if not actually realized, is imminent.

It would be foolish, if our intention were to secure general agreement, to attempt to specify just what progress in moral philosophy would be. It is important, rather, and this perhaps is all that should be undertaken, that efforts be made to encourage those whose competence has been established to address themselves to the problems of moral philosophy. Equally, it is important that inquiry thus encouraged be expended not upon the all too familiar question as to how inquiry should proceed, but upon the substantive problems of moral philosophy. It is one of the peculiarities of the philosophic enterprise that it can, and unless care is exercised will, exhaust itself in philosophizing about itself, its procedures, and its goals to the neglect of those questions without which there can be no philosophy and no philosophizing at any level. This is not to say that talk about how to do philosophy is impertinent or unhelpful. There are times, particularly when our most strenuous efforts to resolve our perplexities fail in their purpose, when we do need to take stock of what it is that we are about and how best to attempt to achieve our goals. But, except in such moments as these, the familiar talk about how to conduct philosophic talk might well be restricted to editorial asides or reminders.

It was with the view of promoting inquiry into the problems of moral philosophy that the idea of a volume of essays first came to my mind. The time did seem ripe to encourage philosophers to explore specific problems in moral philosophy rather than the usually tiresome and surely parasitic question of how moral philosophy should be done. The essays included here were written for this volume, and they are addressed to some of the perennial problems with which moral philosophers have been concerned. Whether or not they provide solutions (and surely it would be too much to expect general agreement on this score with respect to any philosophical essay in any field) they are nonetheless of interest, and they are presented in the expectation that they will stimulate further reflection. Some names familiar to readers of the philosophical literature are missing from the list of contributors, for it was not possible to secure essays from all those who on the basis of past performance could have been expected to say things of importance. Nor is it the case that the philosophers represented in this volume exhibit any single philosophical orientation, style, or allegiance. To be sure they attempt to avoid the familiar vice of vague and general discourse about morals, and they do concern themselves in their several ways with specific problems and with more than a cursory eye to relevant details. But the essays in this volume constitute no illustration of a single way of doing philosophy and provide no basis for any dramatic manifesto. They are offered here without any pretense that they contain any new key to old puzzles and only for what they are worth, as the careful efforts of those who in their different ways attempt to advance the cause of moral philosophy by discussing competently and interestingly some of the important questions of that field.

Compare, for example, the paper by A. N. Prior with, say, those by G. E. Hughes and Gilbert Ryle. The first might well dismay moral philosophers easily disturbed by any of the notations employed by logicians, yet it is precisely in order to exhibit the applicability of the formal procedures of deontic logic to the elaboration of the logical connections between moral concepts that Prior discusses some very recent work in deontic logic and the intriguing problems of interpretation that have arisen. By contrast, Ryle's essay like that of Hughes is studiously contrived to avoid the use of any technical terms, logicians' and nonlogicians' alike. Both endeavor to lay bare the logical bones of the ideas with which they are concerned, not even by attempting definitions, but by more indirect methods. Ryle attempts to throw light upon what is involved in the notion of knowing right and wrong, by examining the respects in which it is absurd to speak of forgetting the difference between right and wrong and also by noting some of the respects in which the knowledge of right and wrong can be compared and contrasted with several distinct things with which it is likely to be confused. And Hughes attempts to explain moral condemnation (as applied to actions) neither by reference to some encapsulated process or emotion occurring when one morally condemns nor by means of a summary formula or definition, but rather by exhibiting the ways in which whatever one does when one condemns is subject in principle to challenge and is capable of being rationally sustained. In developing his account, Hughes touches upon themes upon which other contributors focus their attention —the appeal to the consideration that similar cases are to be treated in similar ways, by reference to which, according to Marcus Singer, moral rules may be justified and the occasional conflicts between them resolved, and the conception of moral blame to which Richard B. Brandt addresses himself in his essay. Thus, in a manner which contrasts sharply with the formal procedure adopted and explicitly advocated by Prior, other contributors in deliberately informal ways seek to disclose the logical connections that hold between crucial moral terms.

It is important that we notice the remarkable manner in which the topics of the several contributors are interconnected. The paper on moral condemnation is really concerned with action of which one disapproves (no doubt the term "condemnation" is too strong a term to apply to the general run of minor moral failures), and there are important logical connections between the notion of an action's being wrong and the notion with which Brandt is concerned, namely, the moral blameworthiness of agents, even though it is not every case of the former that warrants either pronouncing or thinking the agent blameworthy. For, as Brandt makes abundantly clear, the notion that an agent is blameworthy seems to involve the thought that the agent's character is defective, and it is at least doubtful that defective moral character is signified by every wrong act. To recognize these interconnections is to have the subject opened up, to recognize the complexity of the logical connections between our everyday moral concepts.

This, I believe, is the thought behind William K. Frankena's proposal that, instead of employing indecisive arguments pro or con a supposed intimate or internal connection between obligation and motivation (an issue of which Frankena finds distinct traces in Aristotle's criticism of Plato's

conception of the Form of the Good), philosophers conduct
an inquiry along a broad front, coming to grips with, among
other matters, "the nature and function of morality, of moral
discourse, and of moral theory," the relation of moral to other
social functions and practices, with epistemology and even
with psychology, particularly in so far as the latter deals with
human motivation. For the arguments contrived in order to
show that motivation is somehow "internal" to obligation
are, as Frankena clearly shows, far less the knockdown ham-
mer blows they are commonly supposed to be—too often too
much is assumed or presupposed by those engaged in the debate and only a little ingenuity is needed in order to rebut the
formal arguments of one's philosophic opponents. So demon-
stration is not enough.

Here as elsewhere the issues in moral philosophy are undoubtedly complex, and every matter seems somehow, at least
peripherally, to connect with every other. But the alternative
to seeking, devising, meeting, and tinkering with the "demon-
strations" of moral philosophers on this or that issue is not
the adoption of a grand strategy in which all issues are to be
engaged at once (on the ground that we can understand nothing fully unless and until all related inquiries have achieved
their objective—but how, if that were so, could inquiry get
started?). And this, surely, is not what Frankena intends at
all, for if we read his paper with profit we shall be suspicious
of the view that progress in moral philosophy is to be secured
even largely by skillful construction of proofs, and equally we
shall be mindful of the complications of the issues of moral
philosophy, the complexity of the logical geography of our
common moral notions which extends beyond the confines
of moral philosophy into epistemology, psychology, and even
the social sciences. But this fact calls not for an inquiry by
means of easy sweeping generalities, but a great multiplica-
tion in the number of inquiries necessary to advance our
understanding in any appreciable way. In the end, progress

in moral philosophy along a broad front in which epistemology
and other branches of philosophy join forces with ethics will
be achieved neither by piecemeal nor by grand-scale demon-
strative arguments, but rather by the careful, sometimes
grubbing, always difficult and frequently exciting labor expended in attending to details—even to the details of the typical cases in which the concepts under examination receive
application.

One more comment. H. L. A. Hart in his discussion of legal
and moral obligation protests against the almost universal
tendency of philosophers to apply terms like "duty" and "obligation" to the whole field of morality. These terms, he contends, apply to only one segment of morality, and to extend
them to the whole sphere of conduct is to blind us to the
variety and complexity of the moral considerations we employ. Similarly, J. O. Urmson in his paper on saints and heroes
argues against the familiar trichotomy of actions as dutiful,
wrong, or permissible. For there are actions that go beyond
duty proper and of which we approve, not as some writers
would have it because the agent being conscientious takes
out moral insurance and in order not to be deficient in his
duty gives more than his full moral measure, but for quite
different reasons. If Hart and Urmson are correct, terms like
"justification," "reason," and their correlatives have not one
but a variety of uses or meanings in our common moral discourse. And this, once more, is to open up the subject by re-
vealing some of the complications too often overlooked by
philosophers who are prone to generalize and thus liable to
ignore the details of the phenomena with which they are
concerned.

A. I. MELDEN

University of Washington
Seattle

Essays in Moral Philosophy

RICHARD B. BRANDT

Blameworthiness and Obligation

A praising statement, or an expression of blame,[1] need not contain any special or particularly "ethical" words. For instance, "His garden is full of weeds" may do very nicely as a blaming statement, in some contexts. Nevertheless there are some expressions whose normal use is to express blame and particularly moral blame: "morally blameworthy," "reprehensible," "morally guilty," "morally responsible" (which is often not just a statement of agency but of liability to censure), "immoral," "morally wrong," "morally bad," "discreditable," "shameful," and so on.

These terms form a closely related family, although they are not just synonyms; there are jobs they have in common, although each can do jobs that most of the others cannot quite do. One of the basic jobs they have in common—or, if one likes, a basic concept which each of these terms expresses, on occasion—is involved in many important philosophical problems. For instance, there are the controversies about the

[1] I shall limit the discussion mostly to blame, blaming expressions, and blameworthiness; but much of what I say could also be said, mutatis mutandis, of praise, praising expressions, and meritoriousness. There are also some points at which the parallel fails in an important way; I shall comment on some of these.

retributive principle: whether punishment is rendered just
only by *moral guilt*. (This has often been conceived to be
something which God, who looks on the heart, can estimate
more exactly.) There are the controversies about free will:
whether a person can be viewed as *morally to blame* for his
acts, if all of them are determined by natural law. Then there
is the question whether "moral obligation" can be explained
by saying that to assert that someone is obligated to do something is the same as to say that he will be *morally blameworthy*
if he fails to do it. These terms are not, of course, just philosopher's terms, much less technical terms in philosophy. They
are common coin with the housewife or with the judge in
criminal courtrooms, who takes moral guilt into account in
affixing punishment. As the British Royal Commission on
Capital Punishment noted: "Offenses of the same legal cate-
gory differ greatly in *gravity* and *turpitude*, and the courts
make full use of the wide range of penalties they have power
to impose."[2]

This common "concept" of philosophical importance is the
object of our interest. It is convenient to treat of it by considering the *expression* "morally blameworthy," although of
course our interest is not in the points which distinguish this
from others of the above expressions. For this expression I
shall try to do three things: (1) explain it, in the sense both
of giving a correct definition reporting the way in which it is
actually used, and of describing what the normal use implies,
expresses, and accomplishes; (2) locate it in a map of moral
language, with particular attention to its relation to important
senses of "duty" or "morally obligated"; and (3) consider
some recommendations for alterations in its meaning, for the
purposes of precision and avoidance of paradox or for other
reasons. In offering a definition, I shall be concerned only
with problems specific to this particular group of ethical

[2] Quoted by J. D. Mabbott, "Professor Flew on Punishment," *Philosophy*, XXX (1955), 261 (italics added).

terms and not with problems common to the analysis of ethical predicates in general; so that in large part the area of controversy between cognitivists, emotivists, and so forth will be avoided in the hope of getting results acceptable to all.

The simplest way to go about this is to consider first a rather popular theory with some forms of which I happen to disagree. This will suggest some points on which a theory must be worked out if we are to have a serious alternative proposal. This theory consists of the following three propositions, or combinations of some variants of them. (1) It is held that to say someone is *blameworthy* for something is to say that it is *right to blame him* (or punish him) *for it*; and that to say someone is *more blameworthy* for something than somebody else is to say that the former is *rightly blamed* (or punished) *more severely* than the latter. (2) It is held that to *blame* someone is essentially (like punishment) to *do* something, like booing, scowling, or upbraiding. As Nowell-Smith has remarked: "Appraising, praising, and blaming are things that men *do* and can only be understood on the assumption that they do them for a purpose and use means adapted to their purpose."[3] (3) It is held that one of these blaming acts is right if and only if it is useful to perform it in the specific case. Or alternatively (and more plausibly), it is held that the blaming act is right if it is *normally* expedient to perform it in cases of the general sort of the instance in question. In other words, a utilitarian view (in one or the other of these two forms) is taken of the rightness of blaming. In summary, "x is blameworthy on account of his act z," is said to mean, "It is right to blame [in the sense of accusing, upbraiding] x on account of z"—and this is combined with a utilitarian view of when it is right to do something.[4]

[3] P. H. Nowell-Smith, *Ethics* (London: Penguin Books, 1954), pp. 249, 301.
[4] See *ibid.*, chaps. xvii to xx generally, especially pp. 265, 271 ff., 296, and 302 ff. For a simpler form, see L. Garvin, *A Modern Introduction*

If one criticizes this theory, particularly in respect of its view of the *meaning* of "blameworthy," as I should do, one must be careful to distinguish two different purposes that supporters of it might have: (1) they might be advocating it as a definition of what people *actually* mean by their ethical terms, or (2) they might be holding that actual meanings are here rather vague, and that the definition in question is a *good proposal* for the use of the terms, which is reasonably close to the vague actual meanings. With these points in mind, I think we may properly urge (1) that their definition departs further from ordinary usage than one we shall consider later, and (2) that there is no good reason for adopting their definition as a standard for the use of these terms, as contrasted with their actual usage. Let us look briefly at all three parts of the theory.

1. Let us begin with the utilitarian aspect. Naturally this is not the place to consider the tenability of utilitarian theory in its several forms. But it is proper to note that there are probably counterintuitive consequences if we assert that degree of blameworthiness is a function of the utility of blaming a person. This is obvious if we adopt that form of the view which holds that the blameworthiness of a person for an act

---

to Ethics (Boston: Houghton Mifflin Co., 1953), pp. 241–44. See also H. Sidgwick, *The Methods of Ethics* (New York: Macmillan Co., 1922), pp. 428, 446, 448; and G. E. Moore, *Ethics* (New York: Oxford University Press, 1949), pp. 116 ff., although Moore says only that to say that an action "deserves" blame is to "imply" that it is right to blame it.

C. L. Stevenson, in *Ethics and Language* (New Haven: Yale University Press, 1944), p. 307, remarks: "An adverse ethical judgment [statement] is a kind of blame, and since blame is a kind of verbally mediated punishment, our observations about avoidability and ethical judgments are literally a special case of what can be said of avoidability and punishment quite generally." F. B. Ebersole makes the same assumption in his discussion of free will, "Free-Choice and the Demands of Morals," *Mind*, N.S. LXI (1952), 235, 248, 250. As we shall see later, an emotive theory is by no means in principle necessarily committed to this particular view of blameworthiness.

is a function of the utility of blaming *him* in all the particular circumstances. But there are probably counterintuitive consequences even if we consider the form of the theory which holds that blameworthiness varies with the utility of blaming in most cases of a similar sort. For instance, a crime like parricide, which people think is highly reprehensible (remember the savage punishment the Romans reserved for parricide!), on the view in question should seem to be less reprehensible than ordinary murder, since ordinarily the offender will be too hardened or too abnormal psychologically to be improved by condemnation or punishment, and the general public is little tempted toward this crime and does not require to be deterred by a show of indignation. The utilitarian seems able to avoid awkwardness here only by urging that it is a good thing that people get indignant with crimes, and that their indignation should be indulged even when it serves no purpose, if no great harm is done! (If the theory being considered adopted a utilitarian *definition* of "blameworthy," using "expedient to blame" instead of "right to blame," then according to it people would be contradicting themselves if they said that parricide was more reprehensible, while conceding that the utility of condemning it was not greater than in the case of any murder.)

These counterintuitive consequences can be avoided simply by dropping the utilitarian aspect of the theory. But the other two theses are objectionable on their own account.

2. As to the first thesis of this theory: Are we really wanting to commit ourselves about the rightness of performing acts of reproof when we adjudge someone blameworthy? Sometimes we do have strong opinions about this, e.g., when we are thinking of a certain public condemnation of a certain junior Senator. But mostly we do not go around informing people of our moral views of their conduct, and should not want to hazard a guess whether it would be right if we did. (I shall say more of this below.) And is it right, or a good thing, for us

to state our views to third parties? Well, perhaps, but we are hardly taking a stand on this when we judge someone to be blameworthy. An act of overt condemnation is an act which requires its own justification distinct, it would seem, from the justification of the claim that someone is morally blameworthy.

3. But, finally, the theory gives us a fatally misleading steer in its proposal about what it is to blame someone, causing us to overlook something very important for our definition of "blameworthy." To be sure, there *are* performances which we can, without misleading, call "blaming performances." And doubtless "to blame" is often used so as to imply putting on one of these performances. For instance, a person emerging from a "dressing down" might well say, "I certainly got blamed for. . . ." But it would be unfortunate to identify putting on such performances as the exclusive reference of "x blames y for z." We shall do well to consider whether there are no other senses of this expression which throw more light on the use of "blameworthy." And it is clear that there are such other senses. For notice how it is natural to say, "He has not said anything to me, and probably nothing to anyone else, but I think he blames me for. . . ." A cool handshake, a reproachful glance, would ordinarily be described rather as symptoms of blaming than as cases of it. And we say, "He blames himself for . . ." without necessarily implying any internal preaching. It looks rather as if "blaming" refers, at least often, to a complex *state* of mind or attitude rather than to an *act*.[5] And, in so far, it need not have a purpose—and all the speculations about the purposes of blaming are irrelevant to it. And further, then, the statement "I blame you" is not

[5] Here "blame" is not the antonym of "praise." "Condemn" or "censure" comes nearer to this. "Blameworthy" is also more naturally applied only to persons for their acts, and, unlike "praiseworthy," much less naturally to traits of mind or performances. In many contexts "praiseworthy" is indistinguishable in meaning from "excellent" or "fine."

necessarily a performatory utterance like "I promise you" but can be what it seems to be, a *report* of an already present fact.[6]

The theory as a whole, then, is not entirely satisfactory. But its theses suggest what has to be done to get an adequate account of "blameworthy." Accordingly, I shall proceed as follows. First, I shall consider further what it is to blame someone in the sense just delineated. Next, I shall propose a definition of "x is blameworthy on account of z." I shall argue that for someone to be blameworthy is for it to be correct, in a sense to be discussed, for persons to blame him in my sense of blaming. In the course of considering this, I shall develop more fully the topic of what blaming *attitudes* are, and whether there are any overt acts whose fittingness is implied by "blameworthy." Finally, in place of the utilitarian theses of the theory just described, I shall formulate some general principles about blameworthiness. This will lead to an attempt to state the relation between blameworthiness and obligation.

I. *What is blaming?* In order to develop our conception of the sense of "blaming" we have indicated, let us consider some typical uses. We begin with some simple, nonmoral cases. (1) "The mechanic blames failure to start on moisture in the plugs." Here what is meant, perhaps, is simply that the mechanic thinks the car would start if it were not for moisture in the plugs. (2) "He blames the car's stalling on the carburetor" seems to say, "He thinks the carburetor is defective, and that, if it were not, the car would not stall." Now consider a case more nearly relevant to our interests, that of nonmoral blaming of a person. (3) "He blames the designing engineer

---

[6] The reader might try to fit the act-theory of blaming to the following statements, drawn from the *Oxford English Dictionary*. Shakespeare: "Goe girl, I cannot blame thee now to weepe. . . ." "That was not to be blam'd on the command of the service; it was a disaster of warre." Jowett: "We blame our fathers for letting us be spoiled." *Fraser's Magazine*: "I call this bad management, and I blame it upon you."

for the collapse of the bridge." Part of what this statement says is, "He thinks that if the engineer had been up to par, a certain untoward event would not have occurred, i.e., the bridge would not have collapsed." To say this is not, of course, to say that he thinks the activities of the engineer were the sole cause; the wind and the properties of the steel had their part to play. Nor does this statement identify the fault of the engineer: whether it was incompetence, carelessness, or something else. But it does say that the blamer thinks the engineer was at fault; it was not that this engineer failed where no one else could have succeeded (as might have been the case in the days when nothing was known of the principles of mechanics, or the properties of materials)—he failed where a standard or at any rate a first-rate engineer would not have failed. Incidentally, one might blame an engineer in this way but concede that his work was admirable in some respects and that he is in some ways a fine engineer: industrious, on time with his jobs, pleasant, and so forth.[7] But is such an imputation of an untoward event to a defect in a person all that is involved in blaming him? There is, of course, a difficulty here of distinguishing between what is asserted and what is merely implied in the context. But at any rate the sting of such imputations is in their influence on estimates of a person's fitness for his social role. Our engineer may lose his post as a result of a re-evaluation of his capacities.[8] Perhaps, then,

---

[7] It may be we do not say, "He blames . . . for . . ." unless there is some doubt who is responsible. Thus we should not say we blame a singer for a poor performance. For who else would be to blame? We might, however, blame a poor performance on the singer's having a cold. If so, we *excuse* the singer from blame. In the case of blaming on a cold, we do not impute a fault to the cold; indeed, if a cold succeeded in impairing a performance, we might say that it was a "really good one."

[8] These consequences are the chief reason why a person offers excuses. Thus our engineer may try to avoid unfavorable estimates—with consequent unfavorable decisions—by arguing that he was rushed to

we should include as part of the meaning of "x blames y for z" the notion that, as a consequence of the causal imputation of an untoward event to a fault, x has less favorable attitudes to y in some respects, or at least that he would think, if the matter were brought to his attention, that less favorable attitudes toward y were justified. At least, this side of matters seems decidedly to be to the fore in such a statement as, "In the circumstances, I don't blame him for telling a lie!"

Is anything distinctive about *moral* blaming? But it may be well, first, to confess that I am being unidiomatic in speaking of either "moral" or "nonmoral" blaming. For we do not say, "x blames y morally for z" in the way we ordinarily do say, "x holds y morally to blame for z." So, we are not following the English usage of "x blames y" when we start talking of a moral versus a nonmoral kind of blaming. Yet it is useful to do this. For we do distinguish the kind of situation in which x holds y morally to blame from that in which x holds y to blame, but not morally. Notice that, if x holds y morally to blame, he will express himself in moral language, for instance, by saying, "It was reprehensible of y to do z"; whereas if he does not hold him morally to blame, he will not express himself in moral language. So it is useful to distinguish moral from nonmoral blaming, even if it leads us to talk unidiomatic English.

What, then, is the difference? In the first place, we must be careful to take the notion of an "untoward event" very broadly; we hold people morally to blame not only for events which are injurious to someone in some way; we may do so just for telling a lie, that is, for some infraction of a moral rule. But there is a second, more important feature of moral blam-

---

meet a deadline, or that he was worried about his wife's illness, or that the problem in question was assigned him over his protests that his training and experience were in a different field, even if he admits that it was his mistake in computation that caused the trouble.

ing, which clearly is distinctive. We speak of "moral blame" only when the fault to which an untoward event is imputed is of a particular kind: a fault of character.[9]

We should notice that, if moral blaming always imputes something to a fault of character, it need not thereby always impute it to a fault of motivation. Certainly this is true if we define "motivation" narrowly as a disposition for one's behavior to be activated or controlled by expectations of certain consequences of certain possible acts. (When we say, "I wouldn't have done that if I hadn't believed it to have x-effect," we are witnessing to the fact that our behavior was controlled by such an expectation; hence by definition we are witnessing to the fact that the x-effect was a motive of our behavior in this case and also to our being disposed to be motivated by this consideration.) For sometimes the fault of character to which we impute an untoward event is not a disposition to be activated by certain expectations, but the *absence* of any disposition to be activated by them. Or we may think there is something wrong because it did not occur to a person that his act would have a certain consequence, although this would have occurred to most people. Therefore, if we wish to claim that a person is blamed morally only when there is a defect of motivation, we must define "motivation" broadly, including both the absence of motivation and the relative degree of motivation, and such as may be exhibited in deliberations and emotions as well as in choices. But, even so, it is still uncertain that we can defend the view that people are blamed morally only when an untoward event is ascribed to a defect of motivation in this broad sense. For it

[9] I shall consider subsequently how "character" is to be defined, particularly because one might wonder if we do not naturally define it as "traits of mind subject to moral praise or blame," which suggests an unhappy circle. For the present, however, I consider it as well enough understood: and as including such traits as conscientiousness, reliability, honesty—although there probably would be felt to be doubt about the status of traits like irritability, persistence, and impulsiveness.

does seem possible that conduct is blamed (or admired) when an event is imputed to the agent's being arrogant, uncooperative, undisciplined, proud, unreasonable, intolerant, and so on; whereas it is not clear that a manifestation of such traits in action is always analyzable as the manifestation of certain motivation even in the above broad sense.[10]

That moral blaming does imply a defect of character is indicated by the excuses with which people meet an expression of it. Suppose we say to a student, "It was reprehensible of your roommate to tell the dean that lie." Of course, the student may defend his roommate by arguing that he in fact met all his obligations: because he did tell the whole truth, or told what he honestly thought was the truth, or was under no obligation to tell the truth because he had been asked an improper question, or because it is good "public policy" for students to stick together. But, if such a defense cannot be made, he can still correctly rebut the charge by saying, "He was so scared he wasn't himself" or, "He spoke without thinking." These remarks, if convincing, would save one from the implication of being the kind of person who deliberately lies to save his skin.[11] Or he can say, "———— was in the room, and he didn't have the nerve to implicate him," thereby implying that in less trying circumstances he might have done better. Or he might say, "Not one student in a thousand would have acted differently, in the spot he was in." This is a substantial point, which has weighed heavily with those appraising soldiers who have given the enemy information after torture. There are many other types of excuse we can appropriately offer in some situations, such as absence of intention, good motive, inadvertence. Most of them function to show that in

---

[10] See Maurice Mandelbaum, *The Phenomenology of Moral Experience* (Glencoe, Ill.: Free Press, 1955), pp. 143 ff.

[11] But, as J. L. Austin points out, it leaves one convicted of a lesser charge. This paper has benefited from Professor Austin's discussion of excuses.

the circumstances the act did not manifest a character worse than standard. And the fact that they are relevant to a charge expressing blame shows (in the absence of any better explanation of why they are relevant) that in moral blaming something is imputed to a defect of character. The nature of the defense makes clear the substance of the charge.

Moral blaming, like nonmoral blaming, also carries with it the sting of unfavorable attitudes in various respects. I postpone discussion of this point in order to treat of it more fully at a later stage.

For x to blame y *morally* for z, then, I suggest, is for x to charge an untoward event to a defect of y's *character*; and it is also for x to take a correspondingly unfavorable attitude to y—or at least for x to view such an attitude as justified. Whether the unfavorable attitudes characteristic of moral blaming are distinctive, we shall consider later.

II. *The meaning of "morally blameworthy" and its place in a map of blaming language.* Let us now turn to the object of our primary interest, the working of the term "morally blameworthy."

What do we *mean* by "morally blameworthy"? Naturally it will not be easy, in this case, to distinguish what is meant from what use of the term implies.[12]

No definition of this term is satisfactory, we should note, if it does not enable us to state a comparative form; for it is an essential feature of our term that it is possible to say that one

---

[12] In asking about the meaning of this expression, I am looking for an expression synonymous in the sense outlined in a paper, "The Status of Empirical Assertion Theories in Ethics," *Mind*, N.S. LXI (1952). See especially pp. 464–68; also my *Hopi Ethics* (Chicago: University of Chicago Press, 1954), pp. 83–85. In this case, since we are not looking for a complete analysis but one neutral as among various metaethical theories, we may hope to find an expression not only synonymous, in the above sense, but related to it by a linguistic rule, at least of a weak sort (see "The Status of Empirical Assertion Theories in Ethics," p. 468).

person is *more* blameworthy for a certain offense than someone else is for a different offense. (One basic thesis of the retributive theory of punishment would be meaningless if this were not so.)

Let us take, as the phrase to be defined, "x is blameworthy on account of z." There are various definitions that have some plausibility, one of the best of which is the utilitarian type already described. We are also tempted to say that the phrase just means, "x *did z*" in the sense that, if x had acted differently, z would not have occurred. But, if this were so, the kinds of defense already noted as relevant to such a charge would not be relevant. In order to take these defenses into account, we might say, "If x had not suffered from some defect of character, z would not have happened." This particular form, however, along with the previous one, does not admit of a comparative form; and also it seems intuitively clear that our term says something about the propriety of unfavorable attitudes or behavior toward x. These same criticisms are applicable to another which has been suggested: "In producing z, x did not put forth the effort of will to do his duty that he should have." This last, however, is subject to the further objection that we often think a person discredited by his emotions and thoughts, or by other motives or lack of them, different from the will to do his duty. We might follow Russell's suggestion of long ago, which was, roughly: to say that a person is blameworthy for an act is to say that the act is one the agent would have judged wrong after an appropriate amount of candid thought; but among other difficulties is the fact that (as we shall see) an agent's thoughts about his duty are not related as simply as this to the moral quality of his deeds. Again, we might say, "x has failed to do his objective duty in the case of z, and he cannot provide any recognized acceptable excuse, or even an excuse it would be beneficial for society to accept in the long run." This definition is subject to many objections: it must be complicated to allow for a comparative form, and even when complicated has to face the difficulty that there is no simple relation between the degree of blameworthiness and stringency of objective duty. Moreover, the definition should be avoided if possible, because we shall want to define an "excuse" as a statement that reduces blameworthiness; and there are advantages in being able (perhaps) to define "duty" in terms of "blameworthiness."

Rather than consider the defects of these and other possible definitions, it is more profitable to consider a definition that is defensible. I suggest the following, then, as the meaning of "x is morally blameworthy on account of z": [13]

"*Some trait (or set of traits) of x's character was responsible for z in the sense that some trait (set of traits) was below standard,[14] and, all other traits of his personality having been the same, z would not have occurred but for this fact; and it is on this account fitting or justified in itself [15] for x to have some blaming attitudes including remorse [16] toward himself, and for*

[13] There has been a difference of opinion about the values for z which permit the statement to be true or meaningful. For example, can one be blameworthy on account of a trait of character, or only on account of an act or a motive? There will be some discussion of this point later, but I try to frame the definition so that this issue remains open.

[14] We can define "below standard" by reference to attitudes, after the manner of the latter part of our main definition, e.g., as a "trait on account of which, other things being equal, dissatisfaction with a person would fittingly be more severe than it would be for this trait as it is manifested in the character of the average person." We shall see later that, given an assumption about "distinctively moral attitudes," the definition can be substantially abbreviated.

[15] Other things being equal; a factor, independent of any consequences, to be weighed in an over-all appraisal whether the occurrence of such attitudes is good, fitting, or justified.

[16] Perhaps "remorse" is correctly used only for injuries done to another; then substitute "shame" or "guilt." If one supposes that remorse is just retributive indignation toward oneself, we can simply delete the whole clause here, from "for x to" to "toward himself, and," and the following "other."

many [17] *other persons y to have some blaming attitudes in-cluding retributive indignation toward x, and to express them in behavior.*" [18]

The foregoing definition could be transformed into a definition of "x is meritorious (or, perhaps, morally praiseworthy) on account of *z*" by replacing "below standard" by "above standard," putting "feelings of respect" for "blaming attitudes including remorse," and substituting "esteeming attitudes including kindly retributive feelings" for "blaming attitudes including retributive attitudes." We can also define a comparative form: "x is *more* blameworthy on account of *z* than is u on account of *v*." There are various ways of doing this, but perhaps the simplest is to add, after the semicolon, a similar clause involving "u" and "v." Thereafter we make two further changes: (1) after the first "some" we read "more severe blaming attitudes toward himself than it is for u to have"; and (2) after the second "some" we insert "more severe" and then add at the end "than toward u."

Two points in this definition require further discussion. The first of these is the use of the term "character," which may be felt to be circular, since "character" is perhaps most naturally defined as those traits possession (or nonpossession) of which is either morally praiseworthy or blameworthy. (We are not, of course, trying to avoid ethical terms altogether in the definition, allowing "fitting or justified.") A circle here can be easily avoided if we can properly speak of "distinctively moral" blaming feelings or attitudes in the latter part of our definition, for then we can drop "character" for the broader term "personality," since presumably a distinctively moral feeling will be fitting only on account of an act for which

---

[17] We might say "all." But perhaps some persons, e.g., a man's wife, ought never to have such attitudes toward one; or perhaps not everyone is in a position to "cast stones."

[18] I shall discuss later whether the definition should keep the reference to retributive indignation, and also to the expression of anti-attitudes in behavior.

one's traits of character are responsible.[19] Indeed, the recognition of "distinctively moral feelings" would seemingly enable us to drop our first clause altogether. Nevertheless, it seems better to consider what can be done if this simplification is avoided.[20]

One possible way to do this is to follow Nowell-Smith in his suggestion [21] that a trait of character is one that usually has definitely desirable or definitely undesirable effects, and is alterable by praise and blame. But, as he notes, this leads to counterintuitive results. For capacity as a musician and even intelligence have these characteristics but are not traits of character; and it is doubtful whether humility, which is such a trait, has both of them. Nowell-Smith holds that such difficulties do not involve any "major modification" in his theory; but it is not easy to see with what *definition* we are left.

I have no better definition to offer, and therefore propose that we make do with an incomplete but expansible set of necessary and sufficient conditions which serve to specify

[19] A. C. Ewing makes substantially this point in *The Definition of Good* (New York: Macmillan Co., 1947), pp. 154–56.

[20] It is not easy to see how "distinctively moral feeling" can be defined except as a feeling it is proper to have toward a person in respect of his acts expressing his *character*; and, if so, the suggested device will have led us nowhere. It may be urged that it is enough to have named just one such feeling (e.g., retributive anger, remorse), so that we do not have to introduce the expression "distinctively moral" at all. This is true. But some may feel that "retributive indignation" is *never* a fitting attitude to take toward someone; and we shall in any case be defining, later, a term closely related to "blameworthy," in the definition of which "retributive indignation" is definitely not wanted. Well, how about "remorse"? Perhaps the feeling-tone of the emotion called "remorse" is one that appropriately occurs in nonmoral contexts; and, if so, very possibly the term "remorse" involves the notion of a moral context as much as does "distinctively moral." Still, this route may be possible. And anyone who inclines to view the statements, proposed as analytic in section IV, as being synthetic, will have further reason for trying this simplifying device.

[21] Nowell-Smith, *Ethics*, p. 305.

"character" partially. Perhaps, in view of the vagueness of both "character" and "blameworthy," this is as much as we can properly hope for. I propose as *necessary* conditions for being a trait of character that (1) the trait not be a feature of the body (like anemia) and that (2) its manifestation in behavior be subject to voluntary control to a high degree. And I suggest as *sufficient* conditions (1) that its manifestation in behavior be a fitting ground for retributive attitudes; (2) that it be a prime instance of what would ordinarily be called "virtues" or "vices" (such as selfishness, honesty); and (3) that it be a disposition to be concerned or unconcerned about either doing one's duty or meeting some recognized obligation.

The second point of our definition that requires comment is the phrase "fitting or justified." This term means something different from either "praiseworthy" or "blameworthy," and hence its use will not be charged with being circular. On the other hand, it is not, to my mind, an acceptable final terminus in the definition of our terms—for which I should defend a form of the "ideal observer" theory mentioned below—but it has merits for the present purpose, which is to find a formulation that is neutral as among the various warring theories about the analysis of ethical terms. For the phrase does not commit us to any particular analysis, leaving open whether "blameworthy" is to be regarded as naturalistically or otherwise definable. There is another respect in which the phrase is laudably flexible; it admits of, but does not require, interpretation in more than one sense, which is a useful feature if various blaming attitudes are not all fitting in quite the same sense. (But I see no reason to deny that there is a single sense in which all are fitting or justified.)

Let us pursue the neutrality of our definition somewhat further.

"Fitting" can be taken as referring to a nonnatural relation, and hence in principle our definition should not offend nonnaturalists. It is true that it might not satisfy some non-naturalists, who might want to insist that "blameworthy" implies an indefinable quality of badness in addition to the fact that blaming attitudes are fitting in an indefinable sense. But this move seems unnecessary; and we may assume that indefinable notions should be claimed only where definitely required. We must also beware of supposing that any theory is necessarily naturalistic just because the *attitudes* of blaming can be given a naturalistic analysis.[22]

The emotivist, too (but not the pure interjectionist, if we keep our initial clause), can be happy with our definition, if we allow him to have his way with "fitting." For he can say that the definition does not deny any of his main contentions: the emotive meaning or imperative character of ethical terms, his claim that ethical disputes are ultimately disagreements in attitude, and his view that ethical disagreements are not necessarily open to solution by use of scientific methods. Indeed, he may properly welcome our definition, since he himself will wish to mark some difference between "blameworthy" and terms like "good" or "obligatory." And our definition is one possible way in which he can do this; for he will take it as asserting, in effect, that to say, "x is blameworthy on account of z" is to express one's own approval, and to commend to others the approval, of x's feeling remorse on account of z and of other persons' taking and expressing blaming attitudes toward x on account of z.

But neither need a person with sympathies closer to naturalism be dissatisfied. He can define "fitting" in his way. Perhaps he can work out a satisfactory utilitarian definition. Or, following the lead of Professor Findlay, he may say that an attitude is fitting in the sense of "moral" if it is disinterested, dispassion-

---

[22] See H. D. Lewis in the symposium, "The Problem of Guilt," in *Explanation in History and Philosophy* (Aristotelian Society Supplementary Vol. XXI) (London: Harrison & Sons, 1947); also Ewing, *The Definition of Good*, pp. 156 ff.

ate, and reasonable, or informed by a concern for being so.[23] Or he may say that an attitude is justified if an "ideal observer" (perhaps defined in some such way as Professor Firth has suggested) [24] would take it, or approve of it, in the circumstances.

Incidentally, whichever view we take, the recognized excuses will be among the *reasons* we can offer for or against a charge of blameworthiness, in one sense or another of "reason."

Let us turn to some relations between "morally blameworthy" and other blaming phrases. And first let us note that "morally blameworthy" (or "guilty"), although it differs from "legally guilty" in having a comparative form, is nevertheless like "legally guilty" in that it entails that there is no exculpating (as distinct from mitigating) excuse. If there is an exculpating excuse at law—say a plea of self-defense is successful—the defendant is not guilty. Similarly, if there are facts which show that a person's character is altogether free from defect—or that defect is unproved—in the case at hand, e.g., if the agent was acting rightly in terms of the information available to him, then he is not morally blameworthy at all. But to be legally guilty does not rule out the possibility of mitigating excuses: the defendant may bring forward considerations—such as youth, stress of circumstances, previous good conduct—which bear upon the severity with which he may be punished. Similarly, for a person to be blameworthy does not imply there are no mitigating excuses—ones which show that the degree of blameworthiness is low.

To say that someone is blameworthy also *expresses* one's state of blaming him, for one will hardly say this unless one has a blaming attitude or at least takes such an attitude to be

[23] J. N. Findlay, "The Justification of Attitudes," *Mind*, N.S. LXIII (1954), 145–61.
[24] See his "Ethical Absolutism and the Ideal Observer," *Philosophy and Phenomenological Research*, XII (1952), 317–45.

justified. But there are other devices for expressing blaming; and there are statements one can make which imply that someone is blameworthy without saying so. The main reason for this lies in the almost unvarying coincidence of certain types of fact: (1) certain types of act (short-changing the newsboy) almost always show a defective character and almost always are blameworthy; (2) certain types of character are widely disapproved and manifestations of them are almost always blameworthy or thought to be so; (3) in the normal case a failure to fulfill obligations is blameworthy; (4) acts which are blameworthy are normally blamed by those who know the facts, and conversely. (There are also certain words, descriptive of action, which we do not use unless we consider the act blameworthy, such as "cheat," "defraud," "murder.") Thus, by (1), "He told a bald-faced lie" expresses blaming and implies blameworthiness. Or consider, as an instance of (2), "The marriage was a failure because he was selfish from start to finish." Or, as (3), "He plays tennis regularly, but I have never known him to buy any balls." Or, as (4), "His behavior has lost him all his friends." Furthermore, there are statements about "duty" which as we shall see are very closely related to statements about blameworthiness; and there are the near-synonyms we listed at the outset. All of these types of statement, unless further explanations are offered, express blaming and imply blameworthiness. Most of them function more richly than does "blameworthy" itself, which is a pallid phrase. Indeed, we are normally content to imply blameworthiness, and seldom use the word (or its near-synonyms, when they are functioning as synonyms) itself. We use it only in the special cases where the implications of other statements would lead us astray. Thus we might say, "He certainly embezzled the money, but in the circumstances you can hardly regard him as morally blameworthy." "Legally he is to blame, but not morally." (Even here we can use other phrases: "Legally he is to blame, but if you knew the circumstances you wouldn't blame him much.") "Nearly everybody blames him, but he isn't really blameworthy." [25]

One may ask whether there is any normal distinctive purpose of blaming statements—either of the ones which contain an ethical term explicitly, or the factual ones with ethical implications. (One cannot well ask this of private judgments, corresponding statements made in one's head and not aloud —at least, not always or even often. For we are habitually recognizing, judging, and noticing; and these things we mostly do not do for a purpose—but they are rather things we just find ourselves doing, that in a sense just happen to us, although we could avoid doing them if we chose.) The correct answer to this question is: No, it depends on the situation, on the audience we may be addressing. If the person blamed is the person addressed and happens, say, to be our young son, we may well be hoping to modify his general behavior patterns. (E.g., "So-and-so sprained his ankle from falling over the baseball you left on the stairway!") But in this case there may be no definite purpose at all; the angry parent may blurt out a blaming statement with no more than a half-conscious intent to inflict a verbal wound. Or, if the addressee is the culprit but not a close friend or member of the family, the blaming statements may be used to induce him to change a program of action only partly executed; for instance, we may wish an employer to rehire a man whom he has discharged on account of a personal grudge. On the other hand, if our blaming statements are made to third parties, the purpose is apt to be either one of two main sorts: (1) provision of information relevant to action to be taken—as in testimonials, discussions of advancement or demotion, recommendations of suitability as a husband, guest, or tennis partner—and in deliberations about punitive measures

[25] There are also other words we use in blaming expressions, like "unjustifiable," "inexcusable," "intolerable," "bestial," "unbecoming," "coarse," "contemptible," "disgusting," and "indecent."

(whether the culprit should be deprived of his allowance for a week, expelled from college, and so forth); and (2), in the case of talk with family or close friends, simply the comparing of notes, the communication of our opinions and the feeling that these opinions are shared. (Note that we are not usually trying to preach to the recipients of our testimonials, or to our wives and friends!) Perhaps one should add that criticism of others may be ego-inflating and may minister, therefore, to personal needs, although usually not consciously intended to serve this end.

The fact that we do blame people, and that we often express our blame to the culprits or behind their backs, is probably a considerable public benefit. For people do not like the idea of being blamed ·by others, much less having such views expressed either to them or about them. The threat of it acts as a constraint on misbehavior, and as a beneficial one where the acts in question cannot well be prevented by law and in the case of individuals whose interest in doing what is right is weak. In the rough, the practice of blaming—both the state of mind and the expression of it in speech—can be given a utilitarian justification. Philosophers who believe that nothing can be justified at all except in this way will feel more comfortable on this account.

III. *Blaming attitudes, their expression, and the retributive theory.* So far we have said little about the attitudes constitutive of moral blaming, and almost nothing at all about whether certain attitudes are distinctive of moral blaming. We shall now repair this lack. Repairing it will also provide an opportunity to offer examples of blaming attitudes, and expressions of them, which are *fitting*. Both topics can be discussed at once, if we assume that the attitudes and behavior which are normal ingredients in moral blaming are ones which are fitting and justified.

Let us begin with the question what blaming attitudes we think it fitting to *have* toward a blameworthy person, passing then to the question in what way it is fitting to *express* them. There are two cases to consider: the attitudes of the culprit toward himself, and those of other persons toward him. (Actually there are more distinct cases, since we think different attitudes fitting for the culprit's wife or father, or for the victim of an unjust act, his wife and friends, and so forth. But I must ignore such complications.)

The culprit, we think, should (and, if he blames himself, he will) feel guilt, shame, and remorse (not just regret) about his deed; he should be disappointed in himself, angry at himself on account of his deed.[26] (A person may also rightly feel humiliated because others can properly criticize him; but this is another matter.) At least, this is the case if the offense is a serious one. But we also think there is a time when a person may and should forget past lapses.

What blaming attitudes should (and normally do) other persons have toward an agent on account of his deed? First, "prudential" attitudes arising from expectations about future behavior founded in knowledge about the act in question: distrust, lack of confidence, suspicion, including specific attitudes like doubt whether I should enjoy so-and-so as a tennis partner considering his tendency to offer unsolicited advice. (These may be fitting in more than one sense.) Second, antiemotional attitudes of a nonretributive sort, like repugnance, disgust, contempt, and possibly indignation. Hume rightly pointed out that the number of distinct emotional attitudes

---

[26] I do not suggest these are all distinct kinds of experience. "Guilt" seems to be a kind of anxiety, aroused either by the thought of having performed a wrong act (or an act of a certain sort such as stealing) or by the reflection that other persons do or may disapprove of us for our action. I see no reason to distinguish this experience from that of "being ashamed." (We can, of course, *decide* to use these terms in distinct ways, e.g., "shame" to designate the anxiety-experience when aroused by reflections that others do or may blame us.) On the other hand, "remorse" seems to designate either anger at oneself (because I did something wrong that I now wish I had not done, usually because I injured someone), or disappointment at oneself, or both.

of this sort is large. Third, there is retributive indignation, that is, indignation containing some desire for its object to suffer. (Perhaps indignation is always retributive.) Some people feel that retributive anger is never fitting—or even that the first and second types of attitude are not fitting. We shall come back to retributive anger, but surely all these attitudes are frequent or normal components of actual blaming attitudes, in one situation or another. Of these, indignation and remorse have the best claim to be distinctive of *moral* blaming, being suitable responses only to a voluntary act which could have been different if the agent's character had been better; but it is doubtful whether even they are different from nonmoral experiences in respect of noncognitive elements. Perhaps the other attitudes have a distinctive flavor when they are components of moral blaming, partly in that they are founded on a different cognition—distrust or contempt on account of weakness or dishonesty being somewhat different from distrust or contempt on account of unreliability of mathematical reasoning in an engineer. We should note that to say the emotional attitudes are fitting is not to imply that we should dwell on the faults of others; what is meant is that the emotion is a fitting one if the thought of the culprit's deed happens to come to mind. Moreover, we think there is a time when bygones should be bygones, particularly since the guilty individual may have become a different person.

What sort of *expression* of these attitudes do we deem fitting in the case of a blameworthy person? The culprit, briefly, should take stock of himself and consider steps for self-improvement. How about others? An interesting question is whether people in general should join in at least minor forms of punishment: either "speaking to a wrong-doer," as Professor Farmer has said one should, or being pointedly cool, not inviting a transgressor to dinner, and so forth.[27] About

[27] H. H. Farmer, "The Notion of Desert Good and Bad," *Hibbert Journal*, XLI (1942–43), 347–54. H. Rashdall, in *Conscience and*

this we should notice that there are special permissions and obligations for such persons as wives, parents, close friends, perhaps the victim, and representatives of special organizations such as the minister or a member of Alcoholics Anonymous. Furthermore, there are things which a person can show about himself by his conduct that make it impossible for us to act warmly toward him in the future: we shall hardly embrace our old German friend who wholeheartedly assisted in the extermination of Jews or Poles during the war —and much the same if a person offends against us, our family, or friends. But, beyond these and other special cases, it is doubtful whether today—perhaps as a result of city life, or of an attitude of reliance on agencies of law-enforcement —we think individuals are behaving fittingly if they take it upon themselves to stimulate remorse in others, or to inflict any punishment on them. (If someone does take it upon himself, however, we do not think the culprit can complain that his rights have been invaded, except in case, perhaps, his conduct involved only himself.) On the other hand, we should think it unfitting that one should, by word or deed, give a culprit the impression that his deed is condoned, or suggest to him the *absence* of suitably condemning attitudes; but it is not obvious that we think even this unfitting *in itself* (an element that we have proposed is present in the meaning of "blameworthy"), or that we are committing ourselves to this when we say someone is blameworthy. In general, then, it seems that "is blameworthy" does not commit us to claiming the fittingness in itself of any active *antibehavior* on our part.

Nevertheless, this is not quite the end of the matter. If it is fitting in itself to have indignation containing some desire for its object to suffer, then it must also be fitting in itself to feel some satisfaction if the object of the attitude does

---

Christ (London: Duckworth & Co., 1916), p. 146, states that rebuke, protest, showing ourselves hurt, diminution of intimacy may be demanded for the culprit's good.

suffer (and the more so, the stronger the attitude), for it is the reverse side of the coin of desire that one has some tendency to be pleased if the desired event occurs. And this seems to be the germ, at least, of the retributive theory of punishment: the view that (1) other things being equal, it is fitting in itself (as a point to be weighed) for a blameworthy person to suffer for his offense, and that (2) it is fitting in itself that the amount of suffering imposed should correspond with the moral gravity of the offense.[28] Moreover, our view about "blameworthy" implies that these propositions are *analytic*. (If the reference to "retributive indignation" were dropped from the definition, one could still keep them as synthetic.) Of course it is only the *germ* of the retributive theory; for it does not commit us to holding that moral blameworthiness is the only, or even a particularly important, reason for punishment. For this reason also it is not a relevant criticism here that it is difficult to know how blameworthy a person is, in part because it is not easy to know what his state of mind was when he acted; or that the state should sometimes punish irrespective of moral blameworthiness—as in the case of the would-be assassins of President Truman, who may have been motivated only by lofty patriotic motives.

Is this consequence any objection to our definition? Well, it would be if people do not *think* it fitting to feel some satisfaction at the thought of a person's suffering, *qua* perpetrator of a foul deed. (It is irrelevant here whether it *is* actually fitting.) Notice that there is here no inconsistency in *also* thinking it fitting for a person to feel some (even quite strong) *dissatisfaction* at the thought of a person's suffering, when one thinks of him just as a human being, and thinks of how hor-

[28] See C. W. Mundle, "Punishment and Desert," *Philosophical Quarterly*, IV (1954), 221. Mundle, however, holds that these propositions are synthetic, whereas on the theory we are proposing they are analytic. See also C. K. Whitely, "On Retribution," *Philosophy*, XXXI (1956), 154–57.

rible punishments frequently are.[29] The defenders of the
utilitarian analysis mentioned at the outset might attack our
view on the ground that when we think someone is blameworthy we do not think it fitting *in itself* to take some satisfaction in his suffering, *qua* perpetrator of a deed, but rather
think only that it is fitting to take such satisfaction in view of
the *total effects* of this attitude in *most* cases of the sort in
hand (or most cases of moral offense). But it is doubtful if
they can find convincing evidence for this. Their view is probably stronger if offered as a *proposal* for a *better use* of "blameworthy," perhaps in view of the fact (if it is a fact) that a
retributive desire is *not* fitting in itself, whatever people may
think about it. (They might go further and argue that no *antiattitudes* of *any* sort are intrinsically fitting on account of a
person's deeds; the adoption of a corresponding definition
would certainly be a substantial departure from the present
use of our term.) The question whether the actual use of
"blameworthy" should be changed is of course an ethical
question, and the considerations on each side—such as the desirability of more emphasis on future consequences, and the
desirability of not discouraging natural indignation at wrongdoing—are fairly well known.

Nevertheless, one modification in our language habits does
seem to be called for in the interests of clear thinking. For
there are some things, on account of which we *think less* of a
person, which we do not regard as sufficient reason for indignation, whether retributive or not, being fitting. Consider some
things Robinson Crusoe might have done: he might have
drowned his sorrows in drunken debauches; he might have
neglected his mind; he might have committed suicide; he
might have misbehaved sexually with the animals. Most people will think that at least some of these actions would be dis-

---

[29] For evidence of the retributive elements in actual moral thinking,
see F. C. Sharp and M. C. Otto, "Retribution and Deterrence in the
Moral Judgments of Common-Sense," *Ethics*, XX (1909–10), 438–53.

creditable, reflect unfavorably on Crusoe's character. Yet we should not now suppose that indignation is fitting in respect of these offenses, much less that Crusoe should have been punished for them. Again, we may think less of a person because of information about the kind of character he has, without having any information about specific offenses; and conceivably we could have good reason for thinking a man cowardly even if he had never acted so.[30] But we should hardly think indignation fitting on that account, and certainly not punishment (although, in view of the statements of some theologians, we should perhaps not claim unanimity here). Generally, we think these proper only for *acts*.[31] Yet, what are we then to say of these things? If we are careful, we shall not say they are *blameworthy*. Well, we can say what we just said: that they are things which make us think less of a person. But, if we want a special term, why not take "morally bad" and assign it to this job, defining it in the same fashion as "morally blameworthy" except for the omission of reference to all retributive attitudes, indignation, and perhaps best also remorse? (And correspondingly for "meritorious" and "morally good.") This move would correspond fairly well with the natural use of these words and marks a distinction needed by moral philosophy, as Rashdall indicated many years ago.[32]

[30] From tests such as some personality theorists are now experimenting with. Stuart Hampshire, in an article "Dispositions" in *Analysis*, XIV (1953), 5–11, held that this is impossible, since what disposition statements mean is a "summary of a trend" of past behavior and calculations (p. 9).

[31] There is a paradox here. For it is odd that, of two persons with identical character structure, one should be blameworthy, the other not. On what ground is this distinction made? Apparently the only difference is the accidental fact that opportunity has brought the character of one person into action.

[32] H. Rashdall, *The Theory of Good and Evil* (2 vols.; 2nd ed.; London: Oxford University Press, 1924), II, 24. Perhaps we should mark similar distinctions in connection with "moral blaming" discussed in section I.

IV. *The principles of moral blameworthiness.* At an earlier stage a promise was made to consider some common-sense principles about blameworthiness. Let us now formulate some of these and consider how our definition fares in view of them. Our definition, be it noted, should make it formally contradictory to deny any principles (when the *definiens* has been substituted for the *definiendum*) which there is good reason to count as being analytically true.

Whether they be analytic or synthetic, it is clear that we do accept various general principles connecting moral blameworthiness with other features of actions or situations. We "accept" them in the sense that our judgments about particular cases correspond with them (that is, these principles can be got from our particular judgments by substitution of variables for proper names, for example); and in the sense that honest and reflective people will respond affirmatively if such a principle is explicitly put to them for appraisal. The epistemological status of these principles does not appear prima facie to differ from the status of principles of obligation.

These principles appear to fall into several groups. Let us consider some of these groups.

First, consider the principles, "A person is not morally blameworthy for an accident" or "for consequences which he did not anticipate and which he could not have been expected to anticipate" or "for failing to do the impossible." Now I suggest that these have a right to be called analytic (or, if one prefers, quasi-analytic), like "A person ought to do his duty." Correspondingly, our definition makes it formally contradictory to deny them and renders the point of contradiction explicit—for, according to our definition, a person is blameworthy for an event only if it can be imputed to his character in the sense that it would not have happened had some defective trait been different.[33]

---

[33] If one is not impressed by the claim to analyticity, this is reason for dropping the first clause of our definition and following the simplified

Next, consider the principles that a person's blameworthiness is reduced if he acted in a state of confusion, fright, or illness; or if there were conditions of strong and unusual external temptation; or if the positive motives were good ones; and perhaps on account of youth. What do these have in common? Unlike the previous principles, they do not concern conditions in which an act cannot be blameworthy at all because the event cannot be imputed to a defective trait of character; it is not true, for instance, that yielding to a strong and unusual temptation cannot be imputed to one's character—for, if one's character had been better, one would not have yielded. Nevertheless, there is some similarity to our first principles; for the circumstances in question all tend to show that one's action is not necessarily *representative* of one's character, in the sense that they tend to show that it is an open question whether under normal (adult) conditions the action would have occurred. They look like special cases of a general principle that an act is less blameworthy if it is probably not *representative* of one's character. Are there intuitive grounds for taking them to be analytic? I am inclined to doubt it; and therefore our definition is so devised that it is not contradictory to deny them.[34]

---

line indicated previously. On the other hand, one who thinks the simplified procedure difficult has so much the more reason for making the above principles analytic—at least in the sense of recommending that they be so.

[34] We could reach another conclusion. Suppose we held (following the lead of a slightly different proposal by Stuart Hampshire, "Dispositions") that a "trait of character is a disposition to behave or be motivated in a certain way in the *normal situation* or over the *vast range* of situations"—and interpreted "trait" in our definition in this way. (This would not break with linguistic convention. For note how we may hold that a single dishonest act, in extreme circumstances, does not show the agent to be dishonest. We should rather say that he acted "out of character.") Then we could hold that in these circumstances an event or act cannot be imputed to a trait in the sense required; and we should conclude that these principles are analytic, according to our

But there are still different principles. For instance, we think murder more blameworthy than a minor theft; or, perhaps better put, we think a manifestation of disregard for life worse than one of disregard for property (the other motives being equal). Or perhaps we think that, other things being equal, the degree of blameworthiness varies with the degree of stringency of objective duty ignored. (These principles give some point to the *lex talionis*.) And some have urged that there is a correspondence between degree of blameworthiness and lack of conscientiousness, as shown by failure to make the moral effort requisite to doing one's admitted duty.

Are such principles analytic or quasi-analytic? One must concede that some of them are matters of strong commitment; but I can see no ground for claiming that any of them is analytic.

There is one alleged principle of blameworthiness that is of especial interest: the principle that, if an act is causally determined, its agent is not blameworthy. Let us look at this suggested principle on the assumption that our definition of "blameworthy" is correct. (Perhaps we should note that by our definition agents would never be blameworthy on the libertarian's assumption, if what he claims is that traits of character are not responsible for actions!) First, then, I see no reason for thinking that, by our definition, this principle is either analytically true or self-contradictory. Furthermore,

definition, like the first set of principles. According to my definition, however, in this case the agent would not be blameworthy at all, which strikes me as counterintuitive and requiring an alteration somewhere.

My proposal is quite different from that of C. A. Campbell who, in *Scepticism and Reconstruction* (New York: Macmillan Co., 1931), pp. 250–56, suggests that such considerations are mitigating because they are relevant to an estimate of the degree of effort of will manifested by an agent in the action in question; but his theory does not explain all of the examples cited.

we may note that causal determination obviously does not rule out the fittingness, in *some* senses, of *nonmoral* blaming. The question whether determinism rules out *moral* blameworthiness is then the question whether moral blaming attitudes, such as contempt or disgust or indignation or remorse or especially retributive indignation, are fitting in themselves, in at least some sense or other, if the agent's act was determined. But why should they not be? In particular, it is not obvious that the attitude of retributive indignation is not fitting, if we adopt, as I incline to do, an "ideal observer" analysis of "fitting," with the consequence that the question is whether an ideal observer would feel (or approve) any retributive indignation in view of the fact of determination by causes. (Of course, it is possible that this attitude is never fitting irrespective of determinism!) Consequently, even if determinism is true, it is not yet a closed issue whether persons are blameworthy as that term is here analyzed. (Philosophers who incline to agree preanalytically will find this another point in favor of our definition.) Thus some philosophers certainly have been premature in their claim that if determinism is true one can say that people are blameworthy only in the sense that it is expedient to punish or censure them.

V. *Moral blameworthiness and moral obligation.* If we use "moral obligation" in that sense in which it is synonymous with "duty" (and not as when we speak of "*an* obligation" or "*some* obligation"), then there is undoubtedly a close connection between being morally obligated (or having a duty) and being blameworthy.[35] Let us therefore consider their relations

---

[35] Some philosophers believe that the tradition here incorrectly regards the ordinary uses of "duty" and "obligation" as much less specialized than they actually are. With some qualifications I agree with the tradition, but there is no space to discuss the reasons. For a review of the various senses these terms have been held to bear, see W. K. Frankena, "Obligation and Ability," in *Philosophical Analysis*, ed. Max Black (Ithaca: Cornell University Press, 1950).

and possible mutual interdefinability. There is not space to consider all the senses of "duty" or "moral obligation" common in moral discourse; I shall concentrate on two important senses.

Various philosophers have urged that we miss the heart of the concept of moral obligation (reducing it to a mere "it would be better if . . .") if we overlook the fact that a person who fails to do his duty is morally blameworthy on that account. There is certainly a great deal of truth in this, a truth reflected in the fact that moral philosophers, in doubt whether one really has a moral obligation to do something, often settle the matter by asking themselves whether we should *blame* a person if he did not do it. It rather looks as if to say that something is someone's duty is to give notice that his character is on the line, that failure to perform will be on pain of reflection on his character. (This leaves open the possibility that he might be subject to criticism even if he *does* do it.) Of course, if this is true it must be true despite the fact that the two terms normally have very different roles: that one's duty is what one should *accomplish, aim at, or set oneself to do,* whereas "blameworthy" is ordinarily an appraisal word, characterizing a whole situation including the motives, feelings, and so forth. (Yet "blameworthy" may be used as a directive: "You'll be morally to blame, if you don't do this!")

The connection seems closest with what has been called the "putative" sense of "obligation," so let us begin here. I do not know how to identify this sense better than by an illustration. Suppose I say to a conscientious objector, "It is your *duty* to follow your conscience"—something I might say even if I thought that his duty (in another sense) was to join the armed forces. A. C. Ewing says, apparently of this sense, that not to do what one ought in this sense is "always morally blameworthy." Indeed, he goes on to suggest that "*x* is morally obligatory" in this sense can actually be *defined* as meaning, "if the agent were not to do x, he would be morally blame-worthy on that account." [36] Ewing also says something further: that it is a synthetic a priori truth that "I ought to do (in this sense) what I believe I ought to do (in another sense)." Indeed, he says that this sense of "ought" or "obligated" *presupposes* another sense, for, "if I am to be morally bound to do" an act, in *this* sense, I must first believe I ought to do it in another sense. A similar view has been held by many philosophers.[37] But there are serious difficulties with this second contention of Ewing's. For a soldier under torture might well be convinced that he was obligated not to give any information, no matter how unimportant, no matter what; but I do not see that his conviction on this matter is sufficient to make it morally obligatory in this sense. Surely we should not condemn him if he gave some information. Moreover, we might say that a person *was* obligated to do so-and-so, in our sense, even if it had never occurred to him that he had such an obligation, if the fact of the obligation would have been obvious to a morally sensitive person.[38] So I incline to think this sense of "ought" does not *presuppose* any other sense; and I doubt whether there is *any* ordinary sense of "morally obligated" which is related to the agent's opinions about what he ought to do, in the simple way suggested. We can agree, however, that the fact that a person thinks he is obligated to do x is a

[36] Ewing, *The Definition of Good*, pp. 120–21, 130, 168–71. He is very tentative about the suggested definition, but not about whether "obligatory" in this sense applies only if the agent is blameworthy if he fails to do what he ought. (Notice that the definition does not say, "if and only if.") See also W. D. Ross, *Foundations of Ethics* (Oxford: Clarendon Press, 1939), p. 163.

[37] See Frankena, "Obligation and Ability," p. 170.

[38] See Jonathan Harrison in the symposium, "When Is a Principle a Moral Principle?" in *Belief and Will* (Aristotelian Society Supplementary Vol. XXVIII) (London: Harrison & Sons, 1954), p. 114. And, for a slightly different view, Bertrand Russell, "The Elements of Ethics," sections 19–22, reprinted in *Readings in Ethical Theory*, ed. W. S. Sellars and J. Hospers (New York: Appleton-Century-Crofts, 1952).

fact strongly and favorably relevant to its being his duty in this first sense.

But to return to Ewing's major contention, that "A is morally obligated to do x" is logically equivalent to "A would be morally blameworthy if he failed to do x." One might, of course, deny the logical equivalence but still admit to a material equivalence. But is even this the case? There is reason to doubt it. For consider W. D. Ross's suggestion that a person may sometimes be too *kind* to do his duty.[39] In this case, will the person be morally blameworthy at all? And the same will be true, I think (and certainly if our definition is correct), whenever the reason for a person's failure to do his duty is not a *defect of character*. Admittedly, when we are thinking of "duty" in this sense, the occasions on which this is possible will be rare.

Of course, there is no general simple connection between "duty," in this first sense, and "blameworthiness" (and Ewing's definition does not claim that there is). There is reason to doubt correspondence of degree of duty with degree of blameworthiness if one fails to do one's duty, since various circumstances which tend to mitigate blameworthiness are hardly relevant to degree of obligation—for instance, the strength of temptation. Again, a person can be blameworthy for an act that fulfills a duty, if he acts from a bad motive. For example, if an instructor fulfilled an obligation in this sense to report a case of cheating, but did so only because he disliked the student involved, we should think less of him for fulfilling his duty, not more. And we argued earlier that we may think less of a person for manifestations of character defect different from objectionable motivation, and a fortiori different from deficiency in motivation to do one's admitted duty.

Let us now turn to a second sense of "morally obligatory,"

---

[39] *Foundations of Ethics*, p. 167. See also E. F. Carritt, *Ethical and Political Thinking* (Oxford: Clarendon Press, 1947), pp. 26–27.

which we may identify as that sense in which the term is being
used if we say, "You really did borrow ten dollars from him,
whether you remember or not, and therefore you are morally
obligated to pay him ten dollars." (It is here assumed there
are no conflicting obligations or incapacities.) Or, "It seems
to me that probably my duty is to do. . . ." This identification leaves open the question which one of two different senses
is being used, but I propose to ignore this difference. It has
sometimes been suggested that this use is not strictly one of
"*moral* obligation" at all, but surely the belief which we say
bears so strongly on whether I am to blame for failing to do
x is the belief that I am morally obligated to do *x*, not just
the belief that it would be fitting for me to do *x*, or even unfitting that I not do *x*. (Unless "fitting" is being used in a
peculiar sense; but, if so, there seems no gain in clarity by
using it.)

What is the connection between "morally obligated" (or
"duty") in this sense and "morally blameworthy"? Can we
define the former in terms of the latter? It seems not; for the
connection between our terms and "obligation" in this sense
is looser than it was in the preceding case. We saw previously
that occasionally a defense can be put up against the charge
of blameworthiness even if one has not done his duty in the
first sense. This same defense can be used also if one has not
done his duty in the second sense; but there are further defenses which cannot be used with "duty" in the first sense.
For there may be nonculpable ignorance of fact or nonculpable mistakes in judgment or, possibly, nonculpable idio-
syncrasies of moral principle; and in these cases it will be possible for a person to make a mistake about what his duty in
this sense is (or, possibly, correctly conclude that something
is his duty which others can correctly conclude is not his
duty), and then we shall not regard him as morally blameworthy even if he has failed to do his duty in this second
sense. (He may also fulfill his obligations in this sense by

accident, or from bad motives, or in the belief he is doing what is wrong; and in any of these situations he may well be blameworthy.) Thus a *definition* of "duty" or "moral obligation" in this sense in terms of "morally blameworthy" seems out of the question. Doubtless we can frame some true general statements relating the two concepts. For instance, perhaps we can say that, other things being equal, the stronger our objective obligations, the stronger the blameworthiness if we fail (although of course the blameworthiness may be nil if we are ignorant of the obligation, irrespective of how strong it is). And, perhaps, if "morally obligatory" cannot be defined by means of "blameworthy," it can still be defined much in the way the latter term can be—for instance, by the notion of the fittingness (in some sense) of *feeling* obligated to do something.[40]

[40] This paper was read (in substance) before the Fullerton Club in October, 1955, and before the Princeton University Philosophical Forum in November, 1955. I am grateful for the criticisms and suggestions made by members of these audiences and by other philosophers, especially John Mothershead and Roderick Firth.

WILLIAM K. FRANKENA

Obligation and Motivation
in Recent Moral Philosophy

This paper will be concerned with a problem about the analysis of judgments of moral obligation, that is, of judgments in which an agent is said, by himself or others, to have a certain moral duty or obligation in a certain situation or kind of situation. It will not offer an analysis of such judgments, but will occupy itself with a study of a particular opposition between two points of view as to their analysis. The character of this opposition may be indicated as follows. Many moral philosophers have said or implied that it is in some sense logically possible for an agent to have or see that he has an obligation even if he has no motivation, actual or dispositional, for doing the action in question; many others have said or implied that this is paradoxical and not logically possible. The former are convinced that no reference to the existence of motives in the agent involved need be made in the analysis of a moral judgment; the latter are equally convinced that such a reference is necessary there.

Roughly, the opposition in question is between those who regard motivation as external and those who regard it as internal to obligation. We may, therefore, borrow W. D. Falk's labels and call the two points of view externalism and internalism, respectively.[1] It should be noted, then, that the question is not whether or not moral philosophers may or must introduce the topic of motivation. Externalists have generally been concerned about motivation as well as about obligation; they differ from their opponents only about the reason for this concern. Internalists hold that motivation must be provided for because it is involved in the analysis of moral judgments and so is essential for an action's being or being shown to be obligatory. Externalists insist that motivation is not part of the analysis of moral judgments or of the justification of moral claims; for them motivation is an important problem, but only because it is necessary to persuade people to act in accordance with their obligations.

Again, the issue is not whether morality is to be practical. Both parties agree that it is to be practical in the sense of governing and guiding human behavior. That is, it should supply the rules of human practice, and it should not do this out of idle curiosity, but with a real concern for their being followed. But the one party insists that judgments of obligation must be practical in the further sense that their being efficacious in influencing behavior is somehow logically internal to them, and the other denies this. The question is whether motivation is somehow to be "built into" judgments of moral obligation, not whether it is to be taken care of in some way or other.[2]

Here is an old and basic issue. It may be regarded as involved in Aristotle's critique of Plato's Idea of the Good, and is certainly present in Hume's polemic against cognitivists and

---

[1] See W. D. Falk, " 'Ought' and Motivation," *Proceedings of the Aristotelian Society*, N.S. XLVIII (1947–48), 137, reprinted in *Readings in Ethical Theory*, ed. W. S. Sellars and J. Hospers (New York: Appleton-Century-Crofts, 1952). The older term "rigorism" would do for externalism, but it has no good opposite for present purposes.

[2] I owe this use of the phrase "built into" to my colleague C. L. Stevenson.

rationalists in ethics. It is different from, and to a considerable extent cuts across, the issues which have been discussed so much recently (intuitionism versus naturalism, cognitivism versus noncognitivism, humanism versus supernaturalism, relativism versus absolutism, deontologism versus teleologism), for proponents of almost every one of these embattled points of view can be found on either side in this controversy. Indeed, I am disposed to think that it is more basic than most of these other issues, since answers to it are often taken as premises for settling them, for example they are frequently taken by naturalists and noncognitivists as premises for refuting intuitionism.

Yet, ancient and fundamental as it may be, this opposition has seldom been made explicit or studied in its own right, even in recent times when so many of the other oppositions which were latent in earlier moral philosophy have been underlined and debated. Its ghost was raised and given something like form by H. A. Prichard, but only, as he vainly hoped, to be laid forever.[3] R. M. Blake and Falk are perhaps the only others to make a separate study of it.[4] For the rest, however, the opposing positions involved have simply been assumed, it seems to me, without adequate analysis or defense. Hence it is my purpose here to call attention once more to this issue, to consider its present status, and to do something to clarify it and the methods by which it is to be settled.

My sympathies have always been with the first of the two positions described. It has not seemed to me inconceivable that one should have an obligation and recognize that one has

[3] *Duty and Interest* (Oxford: Oxford University Press, 1928).

[4] R. M. Blake, "The Ground of Moral Obligation," *International Journal of Ethics*, XXXVIII (1928), 129–40. Blake was especially concerned about the "internalism," as I call it, of the idealistic ethics of self-realization. See also Falk, " 'Ought' and Motivation," and articles cited below. H. Reiner in *Pflicht und Neigung* (Meisenheim: Westkulturverlag A. Hain, 1951) is dealing with a somewhat different problem.

it and yet have no motivation to perform the required act. But I am less sure of this than I used to be, and shall therefore explore the problem now with the goal, not of arriving at any final conclusions, but of taking some steps in that direction. I shall not proceed, however, by making an independent study of the matter, but by reviewing analytically and critically a number of passages and discussions in the literature of the last two or three decades.

I

Externalism may take various forms, as has been indicated. Intuitionism, holding that obligation is indefinable and non-natural, is the most striking example of it, and internalism has cropped out most frequently in refutations of intuitionism. But many other views have held that moral judgments can be analyzed without any reference to the conations of the agent involved,[5] for instance, any form of naturalism which regards "I ought to do B" as equivalent to "B is approved by most people" or "B is conducive to the greatest general happiness," and any form of noncognitivism which identifies moral requirements with social or divine imperatives.[6] For all such theories, obligation represents a fact or requirement which is external to the agent in the sense of being independent of his desires or needs.

Against them, internalists have a number of arguments which are more or less related and which they usually attribute to Hume, sometimes correctly. It is to a study of these arguments that the first main part of this paper will be devoted. In all of them the theme is that externalism has a

[5] Notice, the question here is about a reference to the interests of the *agent* spoken of, not the interests of the *speaker*.

[6] Not all theological theories of obligation are externalistic, for theologians often hold or imply that "the moral law" is law or is obligatory because it is divinely *sanctioned* (i.e., because it is made to our interest to obey), not merely because it is commanded by God.

problem about motivation, and is therefore false. The first to be considered is an argument by G. C. Field to the effect that, if an obligation represents an external fact about an agent in the sense explained above, then its presence entails no "reason for action." [7] But it is "one of the most deeply recognized characteristics of the moral fact" that it is in itself and necessarily "a reason for acting." Therefore the views of Kant, Moore, and other externalists are false.

We need not question Field's claim (1) that, if an action is obligatory, this is a reason for doing it, since an externalist can accept it. But Field assumes in his discussion (2) that a reason for action is a motive, and this may well be doubted. It seems to me, at any rate, that we must distinguish two kinds of reasons for action, "exciting reasons" and "justifying reasons," to use Hutcheson's terms.[8] When A asks, "Why should I give Smith a ride?" B may give answers of two different kinds. He may say, "Because you promised to," or he may say, "Because, if you do, he will remember you in his will." In the first case he offers a justification of the action, in the second a motive for doing it. In other words, A's "Why should I . . . ?" and "Why ought I . . . ?" are ambiguous questions. They may be asking for an ethical justification of the action proposed, or they may be asking what motives there are for his doing it. "Should" and "ought" likewise have two meanings (at least) which are prima facie distinct: a moral one and a motivational one.

Thus a motive is one kind of reason for action, but not all reasons for action are motives. Perhaps we should distinguish between reasons for acting and reasons for regarding an action as right or justified. It is plausible to identify reasons for acting with motives, i.e., with considerations which will or may move

---

[7] *Moral Theory* (London: Methuen & Co., 1921), pp. 51, 52, 56 f.

[8] Cf. F. Hutcheson, "Illustrations on the Moral Sense" (1728), section 1, in *British Moralists*, ed. L. A. Selby-Bigge (2 vols.; Oxford: Clarendon Press, 1897), I, 403 f.

one to action, and perhaps this is why Field assumes that all reasons are motives, but it is not plausible to identify motives with reasons for regarding an action as morally right or obligatory. At any rate, there is a prima facie distinction to be made between two senses of "ought" and two kinds of reasons, and, if this distinction is valid, then Field's case as he states it collapses. For then an externalist can reply that (1) is obviously true only if "reason" means "justifying reason" and not "motivating reason," and that (2) is true only if "reason" means "motivating reason"; and he may go on to claim that "obligation" is ambiguous, being indeed susceptible of an internalist analysis in its motivational sense, but not in its moral sense. He may even contend that the plausibility of internalism rests on a failure to make this distinction.

The internalist, then, must either show that the above distinction is invalid, which Field does not do, shift to a different argument, or move the entire discussion to another level.

II

W. T. Stace and others use a similar argument against intuitionism and Platonism, contending boldly that, on any such analysis of "A ought to do B," A can admit that he ought to do B without its following that he has an *obligation* to *do* B. Stace's version of this contention may be paraphrased as follows.[9] On an externalist analysis of judgments of obligation, such a judgment merely asserts a kind of fact, simple or complex, natural or nonnatural. Then, even if the judgment "A ought to do B" is true, it does not follow that A has any obligation to *act*, any *practical* obligation, but only an obligation to *believe*. Why should he do anything about B? An obligation to act follows only if A desires to do something about it, and then it follows from this desire alone. Moreover, he may

[9] W. T. Stace, *The Concept of Morals* (New York: Macmillan Co., 1937), pp. 41–43.

not desire to do anything about it, and then he has no obligation of any sort to act. But a moral judgment necessarily entails an obligation to act; therefore externalist theories are
false.

This argument, which seems so plausible to Stace, has always
been puzzling to me. Let us begin, as he does, by supposing
that a moral judgment *is* just a statement of some kind of "external" fact. Then one cannot admit such a fact about oneself, and still ask sensibly if one has a moral obligation to act.
For to admit the fact is then to admit the obligation. One
cannot in that case ask, "Why morally ought I do the act in
question?" except to gain an insight into the *grounds* of the
admitted obligation. One can still ask, "Why should I do the
act?" but only if one is using "should" in the sense in which
one is asking for motivation, or in some third sense. No doubt,
as Stace says, one *will* do it only if he desires to do what has
the given kind of "external" characteristic. Then one's desire
obliges him in the sense of moving him. But the admitted
moral judgment asserts a *moral* obligation nonetheless, and
whether one will in fact perform the act in question or not
does not bear on his having this obligation. Even if one may
not desire to do what is right (i.e., what has the characteristic
referred to by "right" on our hypothesis),[10] this does not
change the fact that one has a moral obligation; it means only
that one has no motivation, at least occurrently. That one has
no moral obligation does not follow unless having an obligation entails having a motive. But this Stace does not show,
and it is obviously true only in one sense of "obligation."

In fact, it is clear that Stace is assuming that to have an
obligation is to have a motive, just as Field did, and his argument is essentially the same, though verbally different. And
again the answer is that, until the contrary is shown, one must

---

[10] That one may fail to feel any disposition whatsoever to do what is
right cannot simply be asserted, for it is to make an important claim
about human nature even on an externalist view.

distinguish between two senses of "should" or "ought." For, if this distinction is valid, it can be claimed that Stace's argument reduces to this: even if I ought in one sense, it does not follow that I ought in the other sense, which is true but refutes no one. Stace, like Field, has failed to observe or consider the possible ambiguity of "should."

What he has noticed is that one apparently can ask, "Why should I do what I morally ought to do (if this represents some fact independent of my interests)?" But one can ask this sensibly only if "should" and "morally ought" are used in different senses. One cannot ask, "Why morally ought I to do what I morally ought to do?" even if "morally ought" does stand for an objective property. But neither can one ask, "Why should I do what I morally ought to do?" if "I should" and "I morally ought" *both* mean "I have a motive" or "It is necessary for my happiness," as they do on Stace's own view. For the question to be sensible, "I should" and "I morally ought" must have distinct meanings, whatever these are; and, while one may entail motivation, the other need not.

III

The fullest and most recent version of this argument is to be found in P. H. Nowell-Smith's book.[11] He remarks with inter-

---

[11] *Ethics* (London: Penguin Books, 1954), pp. 36–43. Nowell-Smith is a noncognitivist, not a cognitivist as Field and Stace are. There are similar arguments in A. J. Ayer, "On the Analysis of Moral Judgments," *Horizon*, IX (1949), 171 ff.; Alf Ross, "The Logical Status of Value Judgments," *Theoria*, XI (1945), 203–8; R. C. Cross, "Virtue and Nature," *Proceedings of the Aristotelian Society*, N.S. L (1949–50), 123–37; H. Reichenbach, *The Rise of Scientific Philosophy* (Berkeley and Los Angeles: University of California Press, 1954), chap. xvii; R. M. Hare, *The Language of Morals* (Oxford: Clarendon Press, 1952), pp. 30, 79–93, 171; and elsewhere. I do not discuss these writers, however, because they may not be advancing quite the same argument; they seem to be insisting not so much that moral judgments are motivating, as that they are prescriptive. Hence they may not be internalists. But, if they are, then what I say will apply to them, too.

est that the intuitionists "have but repeated Hume's argument" about the gap between the *is* and the *ought* in refuting naturalistic theories.[12] Then he goes on to contend that intuitionism itself may be disposed of by essentially the same argument, namely, that it likewise fails to bridge the gap; and in making this striking contention good he elaborates the argument that, no matter what "fact," natural, metaphysical, or nonnatural, one may establish about an action, it will still not follow that one ought to do the action.

> The intuitionist's answer to the question "Why should I be moral?"—unless, like Prichard, he rejects it as a senseless question—is that, if you reflect carefully, you will notice that a certain act has two characteristics, (a) that of being obligatory and (b) that of producing a maximum of good or of being a fulfilment of a promise . . . etc. . . . But suppose all this has taken place. . . . Does it follow that I ought to do the action . . . ? . . . a world of non-natural characteristics is revealed to us by a . . . faculty called *"intuition."* . . . And from statements to the effect that these exist no conclusions follow about what I *ought to do.* A new world is revealed for our inspection . . . it is mapped and described in elaborate detail. No doubt it is all very interesting. If I happen to have a thirst for knowledge, I shall read on. . . . But what if I am not interested? Why should I do anything about these newly-revealed objects? Some things, I have now learnt, are right and others wrong; but why should I do what is right and eschew what is wrong? . . .
>
> Of course the question "Why should I do what I see to be right?" is . . . an absurd one. . . . But . . . [this question], which [is] absurd when words are used in the ordinary way, would not be absurd if moral words were used in the way that intuitionists suppose . . . if "X is right" and "X is obligatory" are construed as statements to the effect that X has the non-natural characteristic of rightness or obligatoriness, which we just "see" to be present, it would seem that we can no more deduce "I ought to do X" from these premises than we could deduce it from "X is pleasant" or "X is in accordance with God's will."

[12] A. N. Prior says that Hume was but repeating Cudworth! Cf. *Logic and the Basis of Ethics* (Oxford: Clarendon Press, 1949), p. 33.

This passage needs discussion here, even at the risk of some repetition. To begin with, it seems to me that Nowell-Smith is confusing two arguments, both suggested by Hume.[13] One says that conclusions involving "ought" cannot be derived from premises involving only "is" and not "ought." The other says something like this: conclusions involving "ought" cannot be derived from premises stating only *truths*, natural or nonnatural, even if one of these truths is what is meant by an ought-statement. Now it is the first of these which is used by the intuitionists against their opponents, and *it* cannot be turned against them. For its point is valid even if ought-statements assert truths as the intuitionists claim, provided only that the truths they assert are different from those asserted by any is-statements. Insofar, then, as Nowell-Smith is trading on whatever validity this argument possesses, his case against intuitionism breaks down. It is the other argument on which he must rely.

This one is harder to deal with. We must first eliminate another point on which Nowell-Smith seems to trade. He supposes that "X is obligatory" stands for a nonnatural property and then argues that it does not follow that I ought to do X. Of course, it does not follow that *I* ought to do X, since it was not specified for whom X is obligatory. Let us take "I have an obligation to do X" instead, and let us suppose that it asserts a fact about me and X, natural or nonnatural. Then the argument is that, even if it is true, it does not follow that I have an obligation to do X. Whether this is correct or not, however, depends on the meaning of "I have an obligation to do X" when it appears after the words "it does not follow." [14]

[13] The famous passage in Hume (*Treatise*, Bk. III, Pt. I, section 1), often appealed to lately, can be read as stating either of these arguments, but they must not be confused. He himself seems to distinguish it from the more obviously internalistic argument given a few pages earlier; hence he may intend it only in the first sense.

[14] As G. E. Moore pointed out in his reply to me, *The Philosophy of*

If it here also stands for the fact in question, as cognitivists'
hold and as we are for the moment supposing, then it does
follow that I have an obligation to do X, for the "conclusion"
simply repeats the "premise."

Nowell-Smith may, of course, reply that no truth, natural
or nonnatural, can entail an *obligation*. My point has been
that it can *if* an obligation is a certain fact, as cognitivists
claim. Nowell-Smith may go on to contend that an obligation
is not identical with *any* such fact, but then he must show this
independently, and cannot do so by the present argument. His
contention may seem plausible when it is applied to naturalistic theories, as intuitionists have always thought. But it is
not obviously true, if one does not identify obligation and
motivation, that an obligation cannot be identical with any
peculiar kind of "fact" such as the intuitionist believes in, for
he claims that it is such a peculiar "fact" precisely to account
for its obligatoriness. He has, as it were, built obligatoriness
into his "fact." Possibly this cannot be done or is too pat a
solution, as Nowell-Smith suggests. But this must be shown
independently; Nowell-Smith must argue directly that such a
fact is inconceivable or is not what is meant by "obligation,"
remembering as he does so the prima facie distinction introduced above. For if it is conceivable and is what is meant by
"obligation," his present argument is not cogent.

The real reason why Nowell-Smith thinks that no set of
truths or facts entails my having an obligation to act is, of
course, the fact that he implicitly assumes that my having an
obligation implies my having a motive. This comes out when
he says about the intuitionist's brave nonnatural world, "But
what if I am not interested?" And again the answer is that,
while there is a sense in which having an obligation equals
having an interest, there is prima facie another sense in which
it may stand for a truth of another kind, natural or not. It is

G. E. *Moore*, ed. P. A. Schilpp (Evanston and Chicago: Northwestern
University, 1942), pp. 567 ff.

true that motivation will not follow logically from this truth
(though it may follow causally from a recognition of it); [15]
it will not follow any more than "Y is a fellow traveler" follows
from "Y is tickled pink." In this sense Nowell-Smith's point
is correct. I can contemplate all the facts pointed out by the
intuitionists and externalists and still ask sensibly, "Ought I?"
if I am asking about motivation. But it may still be nonsense
to ask, "Ought I?" in the moral sense, as the cognitivist would
claim.

Here Nowell-Smith insists that, when words are used in the
ordinary way, it is absurd to ask of an act which it is admittedly right for me to do, "Why should I do it?" And of course
it is, if "should" is used in its moral sense. But in this sense,
the intuitionist may contend, his usage involves no gap either,
as we have been seeing. It is only if "should" is used in its
motivation-seeking sense that he must allow that there is a
gap, and in this sense, he may claim, there really is a gap, which
is not noticed because of an ambiguity in the word "should"
as it is ordinarily used.

Again, then, it becomes apparent that the internalist must
either challenge this distinction between two uses of "should,"
or show independently that "should" implies motivation even
in its moral use.

IV

The internalist arguments discussed above depend on the
claim that obligation and its recognition entail the existence
of motivation, but they depend on it indirectly, through an
identification of a reason for acting, or of an obligation to act,
with a motive for doing so. Frequently, however, the internalists
make this claim in so many words, and conclude directly that externalistic theories are mistaken. Thus Field argues against
Moore that "the moral fact" is in itself and necessarily of

[15] As H. D. Aiken has pointed out. See below.

interest to us when apprehended, but this it cannot be on Moore's view, and therefore Moore's view is false.[16] Likewise for all forms of externalism. Suppose we take Field's first premise in a psychological sense, as asserting (1) that, if one acknowledges an obligation to do something, then it is psychologically impossible for him not to have some tendency to do it, and (2) that his recognizing his obligation by itself produces this tendency. Then it can be denied with some plausibility, for not everyone's moral experience witnesses to the truth of either of these assertions, let alone of both of them. But suppose it is true. Must an externalist give up his position? Only if we can add two further premises: (3) that, no matter what external fact we may become acquainted with, it is always psychologically possible for us to be indifferent to it, and (4) that "the bare knowledge of anything can never move us to action." Now (4) is plausible, as Field shows at some length in attacking "the Kantian fallacy." But most externalists would admit that knowledge can move us to action only by awakening an already existing desire, in this case, perhaps, a desire to do the right.[17] As for (3), it is obviously false, since there are external facts to which, given the conative natures we have, we cannot remain wholly indifferent. And, this being the case, an externalist like Moore might insist that we are so constituted that we cannot be wholly cold in the presence of the particular external fact which he regards as constituting obligation—a claim which Field does nothing to disprove.

However this may be, Field gives us no grounds for accepting his premise that the recognition of an obligation is by itself and necessarily a motive. He seems simply to infer this from the fact that such recognition is by itself necessarily a reason for action. But we have seen that, at least prima facie, "reason" is ambiguous here, and something may be a reason without

[16] *Moral Theory*, pp. 56 f.
[17] Cf., e.g., W. D. Ross, *The Right and the Good* (Oxford: Clarendon Press, 1930), pp. 157 f.

thereby being a motive. Field must then show that his assertion is. true independently of any possible confusion between two senses of "reason," which he does not do. And, if he is not going in for the longer kind of reasoning to be described in our last section, he must show that it is true in a logical sense, as asserting that it is logically impossible to have an obligation to which one is indifferent.

Another use of the argument occurs in C. L. Stevenson's important first article,[18] where he employs it against "any attempt to define ethical terms without reference to the interests of the speaker"—in favor, not of an internalistic cognitive theory, as in Field and Stace, but of an emotive one. Stevenson contends, among other things, that ethical terms "must have, so to speak, a magnetism," and that any analysis of them must provide for this. By saying they have magnetism he means that "a person who recognizes X to be 'good' [or 'obligatory'] must *ipso facto* acquire a stronger tendency to act in its favor than he otherwise would have had." He then writes:

> This rules out the Humian type of definition. For according to Hume, to recognize that something is "good" is simply to recognize that the majority approve of it. Clearly, a man may see that the majority approve of X without having, himself, a stronger tendency to favour it.

The same reasoning, of course, will rule out intuitionism and other forms of externalism. On all such views, to assent to a moral judgment is to assent to a fact which involves no reference to one's interests; therefore this assent does not *ipso facto* or necessarily lead to a stronger tendency to favor the action in question.

This is essentially Field's argument over again, as Stevenson himself recognizes. The crucial premises are two: (1) that anyone who assents to a moral judgment must *ipso facto* or necessarily acquire a stronger tendency to do the action in

[18] "The Emotive Meaning of Ethical Terms," *Mind*, N.S. XLVI (1937), 16.

question, and (2) that assenting to a fact which involves no reference to one's own interests will in no case *ipso facto* or necessarily produce such a tendency. Now these statements may be understood in a *causal* or psychological sense. But, if so, they should be shown to be true before they are used to rule out entire theories. The first is certainly not obvious in the case of all kinds of ethical judgments; it may be true of value-judgments but is it true of all ought-judgments? That it is seems particularly doubtful if we must distinguish between two kinds of ought-statements, for then one kind might be incitive in tendency and the other not; yet Stevenson takes no account of the possibility of such a distinction. Again, as was just said, it is hard to believe that in the case of every "external fact" about an action it is *psychologically* possible for us to be indifferent to it. If this were so we could have no "primary appetites" in Butler's sense; all of our interests would be washing-women taking in each others' laundry. But, if there are interests whose objects are "external," then Hume can plausibly claim that it is a psychological law of human nature that we invariably feel *some* tendency to do what we believe the majority to approve, or an intuitionist that it is psychologically necessary that we pursue a nonnatural right or good, as Plato thought.

Now Stevenson does nothing to refute such psychological theories. He must, then, be thinking that assenting to a moral judgment in some sense *logically* entails its having a tendency to affect one's action—that an analysis of a person's moral judgment or recognition that something is obligatory must in some way involve a reference to his tendencies to do the action in question. That is, motivation must be "built into" the analysis of ethical utterances. This dictum, however, cannot simply be assumed, if the issue is not to be begged, especially if the distinction referred to earlier holds. Moreover, it is ambiguous. It may mean that a reference to the agent's desires is to be built into the *descriptive* meaning of ethical judgments, or it may mean that part of what is meant by *assenting* to a moral judgment is a disposition to respond accordingly. The first of these alternatives is taken by Field and Falk[19] but rejected by Stevenson. The second, as we shall see in a later section, can be accepted by an externalist.

V

A somewhat novel form of the present argument has been advanced by H. D. Aiken in a well-known article.[20] He maintains (1) that judgments of obligation are normative in the sense that they influence the will and determine conduct, and (2) that "the relation between cognition and motivation, on any theory of motivation whatever, is a causal, not a logical, relation"; and he concludes that all "descriptivist" analyses of judgments of obligation are therefore mistaken, whether naturalistic or nonnaturalistic (including internalistic forms of naturalism such as those of Field and Stace). (2) is an important point and needed to be made, but it may be admitted. (1) is a premise already familiar to us in other forms, but, whereas his predecessors regard it as empirical, Aiken makes it analytic. He defines a judgment of obligation as one which influences conduct "by whatever means." This, however, has a curious effect, namely, that what are usually called ethical judgments may not be judgments of obligation in his sense, since they will be so only if they influence the will. But then, even if his argument shows that his "judgments of obligation"

[19] Cf. Also D. C. Williams, "The Meaning of Good," *Philosophical Review*, XLVI (1937), 416–23.

[20] "Evaluation and Obligation," *Journal of Philosophy*, XLVII (1950), 5–22, reprinted in *Readings in Ethical Theory*. See also "The Authority of Moral Judgments," *Philosophy and Phenomenological Research*, XII (1951–52), 513. A similar view is present in A. Moore, "A Categorical Imperative?" *Ethics*, LXIII (1952–53), 235–50, to which my criticisms also apply.

cannot be descriptively analyzed, it proves nothing about the so-called moral judgments with which the rest of us have been concerned.

Aiken is tacitly assuming that judgments of the form "A should . . . ," "B ought . . . ," and so forth, in the uses with which we are concerned, are all causally efficacious, at least normally, and so fall under what he calls "judgments of obligation." This may be doubted, especially if we keep in mind our distinction between two kinds of "should" sentences, but let us accept it for the sake of the argument. Then his conclusion still does not follow. For a judgment that causally affects behavior may be susceptible of a cognitivist analysis, and even of an externalistic one. That is, a statement may be a "judgment of obligation" and yet be descriptive. For its moving power may be due wholly to the information, natural or nonnatural, which it conveys to our desires. If I say to you as we cross the street, "There is a car coming," my statement will influence your actions, and it may do so simply in its informative capacity (given your desire to live). Then it will be a "judgment of obligation" and yet be capable of a descriptivist and externalist analysis.

The matter may be put thus. Consider "I ought to do X" in any safely ethical use. The question is whether or not this is to be given an internalistic analysis. Aiken does give us such an analysis of the meta-sentence, " 'I ought to do X' is normative." But this is not an analysis of the sentence, "I ought to do X," itself, and so all of the standard theories about its analysis remain open. It is, however, this sentence which constitutes our problem; we want to know the function or meaning of "obligatory" as it is used in, "It is obligatory on me to do X," not in, " 'It is obligatory on me to do X' is obligatory." Aiken's attempt to sidestep the dispute about ethical sentences is no doubt a laudable one; the moral of my critique is only that, if one does sidestep it, one must not draw any conclusions about it, as he seems to do.

VI

The above kinds of argument against externalism all depend
on the claim that obligation or judgments of obligation somehow entail motivation, perhaps directly, perhaps by identifying
motivation and reasons for acting or by identifying motivation
and obligation to act. I have tried to dispose of each argument
individually, but my main point has been that there is a prima
facie distinction to be made between moral or justifying reasons and exciting or motivating ones, or between moral and
nonmoral obligation; that this distinction is usually neglected
by internalists when they use such arguments; and that if this
distinction is valid the arguments lose their cogency. For then
the externalist can reply that, while there is a motivational
sense of "ought" which *is* "internal," there is another sense
of "ought" which is moral and which may be "external" for
all that has been shown so far.

In making this point I have but echoed an old intuitionist
refrain, which to my knowledge was first sung by Samuel
Clarke and last by R. M. Blake, but which may also be sung
by nonintuitionists. Clarke, observing the rising conflict between internalism and externalism of his day, distinguishes
"the truest and formallest obligation," which is moral, from
"the Dread of Superior Power and Authority, and the Sanction of Rewards and Punishments . . . which is . . . really
in itself only a *secondary* and *additional* Obligation, or *In-
forcement* of the first." Then he remarks that a failure to notice this ambiguity of the term "obligation" has blinded some
writers to the (externalist) truth that "the original *Obligation*
of all . . . is the eternal *Reason* of Things. . . ." He says
drily, in parentheses, ". . . the ambiguous use of which word
[Obligation], as a *Term of Art,* has caused some Perplexity
and Confusion in this Matter"—the perplexity and confusion
being, of course, in the minds of the internalists.[21] It seems to

21 Cf. *British Moralists*, II, 16.

me, as it seemed to him and to Blake, that neglect of this ambiguity has been a serious mistake in recent moral philosophy.

Even if the distinction is valid, however, it does not follow that internalism is false, but only that externalism may be true if it cannot be refuted on grounds other than those so far considered. One may admit the distinction and still claim that both kinds of judgment of obligation, the moral as well as the nonmoral, are susceptible of an internalistic analysis. In fact, some recent internalists do distinguish moral from nonmoral obligation in one way or another, though apparently without seeing that the above kind of argument does not establish the internality of the moral ought, when this is distinguished from the nonmoral one. It may then be held that, independently of such a distinction and of the above arguments, it can be shown that moral obligation is internal. We must now in the second main part of this paper take up some considerations that seem calculated to show this.

It will be helpful, first, to sort out a number of propositions that internalists have held or may be holding, particularly since they have rarely been distinguished in the literature. All of the above writers, and many others, are convinced that having or acknowledging an obligation to do something involves having, either occurrently or dispositionally, some motivation for doing it; and they infer that externalism is false. But this proposition can be taken to assert several things, namely: (1) that the state of having an obligation includes or is identical with that of being motivated in a certain way; (2) that the statement, "I have an obligation to do B," means or logically entails the statement, "I have, actually or potentially, some motivation for doing B"; [22] (3) that the reasons that justify a judgment of obligation include or are identical with the reasons that prove the existence of motivation to act accordingly; (4) that the reasons that justify a judgment of ob-

[22] Or, "It is to my interest to do B," or, "B is conducive to my self-realization."

ligation include or are identical with those that *bring about* the existence of motivation to act accordingly; (5) that, although justifying a moral judgment does not include giving exciting reasons for acting on it, it presupposes the existence, at least potentially, of such excitement; (6) that *saying* or being *said* to have an obligation presupposes one's having motives for doing the action in question; (7) that *assenting* to an obligation entails feeling or having a disposition to feel at least some inclination to act in the way prescribed; or (8) that one can know or "see" or think that one has a certain obligation only when one is in a favorable conative state with respect to performing the act in question.

Even these formulations are not very rigorous, but perhaps they will suffice to make clearer the opposition we are discussing. The externalist is concerned to deny (1) through (4), which the internalist will assert. If they are true, externalism is untenable. However, as far as I can see, the internalists have not shown them to be true to such a degree that they can be safely used as premises for refuting externalism; indeed, they are plausible only when the distinction between two senses of "ought" and "reason" that we have been stressing is not borne in mind.

As for (5) through (8), an externalist may accept them, though they may also be denied with some plausibility (and would be denied by a really "compleat" externalist). It is obvious that he can admit (8), for it makes only a psychological assertion about the conditions of moral insight; in fact, (8) is maintained by such externalists as Scheler and Hartmann.[23] (5), as we shall see, may also be agreed to by an externalist, though only if "presupposes" is understood in some psychological or "contextual" sense, and not in a strictly logical one.

The arguments to be dealt with here generally involve (1), (6), or (7), and we may take first those that use (1) in some form or other. In one of them Falk appeals to the familiar

[23] Cf. also H. Reiner, *Pflicht und Neigung.*

principle that "I morally ought" implies "I can," adding that "I can" implies "I want to (in the sense that I have, at least dispositionally, some motivation for doing)," and then drawing an internalist conclusion.[24] Suppose we admit, though both claims may be disputed, that "I morally ought" in all its senses implies "I can," and that "I can" implies "I want to." Even then this argument will be cogent only if the "implies" involved is a logical one in both cases. But is it in " 'I can' implies 'I want to'?" To say, "I cannot whistle a tune while standing on my head, unless I feel some inclination to do so," is perhaps an odd thing to say about an odd bit of behavior, but it seems at most to state a physical fact, not a logical necessity. One may, of course, so define "I can" as to include "I have some impulse to," but it is not obvious that one should, and it is not clear that "ought" implies "can" as so defined.

But "*ought* implies *can*" need not be construed as asserting a strict logical implication. It may plausibly be understood as saying: (a) moral judgments "presuppose," "contextually imply," or "pragmatically imply" that the agent is able to act as proposed or is believed to be, but do not assert or state that he is; or (b) the *point of uttering* moral judgments disappears if the agents involved are not able to act as proposed or at least believed to be; or (c) it would be morally wrong to insist that an agent ought to do a certain action, if he is or is thought to be unable to do it. If Kant's dictum is interpreted in one of these ways the externalist need have no fear, for then it will not serve to refute him.

VII

In a somewhat similar argument, Aiken reasons that obligation presupposes responsibility and that this presupposes motivation:

[24] Cf. "Morals without Faith," *Philosophy*, XIX (1944), 7; "Obligation and Rightness," *Philosophy*, XX (1945), 139.

Hume's argument can be stated in another . . . way. We assume that no person can be held morally responsible for actions which he did not willingly perform. We do not address such judgments as "Killing is wrong" to cyclones. . . . In short, we regard only responsible beings as moral or immoral. But . . . responsibility *presupposes* a motive for or interest in any act for which a person is held "responsible." If this is so, the very notions of "moral" and "immoral" involve a reference to feeling or sentiment; and every moral judgment states or implies such a reference.

Aiken then asserts that this argument "disqualifies all theories whatever which . . . deny that moral categories are to be construed in terms of human feeling or interest. . . ." [25] In another place he claims that obligation and desire are intimately related, "For . . . it is doubtful whether the term ['ought'] is ever properly applied to anything save motivated activity." Here too he takes this conviction as a criterion to be met "by any adequate analysis of 'ought'." [26]

Now, the argument from obligation to responsibility to motivation is like the argument from obligation to ability to motivation, and the same points hold about it. Instead of repeating, then, let us take up the conviction that moral obligation and judgment presuppose motivation. It does seem correct to say that my having moral duties implies that *others* have desires and feelings, but this externalists need not deny. It is also plausible to hold that my having duties, or being a moral agent whose acts are right or wrong, presupposes *my* having interests and motives. To this extent Aiken is, in my opinion, correct. But an externalist can agree, and still insist that, although one can ascribe obligation only to a motivated being, to ascribe an obligation to such a being is not to talk about his motives but to assert some external fact about him.

More crucial is Aiken's further claim that A's having an

[25] *Hume's Moral and Political Philosophy* (New York: Hafner Publishing Co., 1948), p. xxxi.
[26] "A Pluralistic Analysis of the Ethical 'Ought,'" *Journal of Philosophy*, XLVIII (1951), 497.

obligation to do B presupposes his having not only interests *überhaupt* but, directly or indirectly, an interest in doing B (though not necessarily a predominant one). If this means that A's having a duty to do B logically entails his having an interest in doing B, or that establishing his obligation to do B logically entails showing him that he has such an interest or producing such an interest in him, it may be denied. A man who is seeking to determine if he has a duty to do a certain deed need not look to see if he has any motives for doing it, and he cannot claim that he does not have the duty simply on the ground that he finds no supporting motivation. Aiken may reply that, nevertheless, A's having an obligation to do B in some sense presupposes his having a concern to do B, at least dispositionally, and I am inclined to agree that it does, but only in the sense that *ascribing* this duty to A "contextually" or pragmatically implies that, if A sees he has it, he will have some concern to perform it (6). This, however, does not mean that A's having this concern is a condition of his having a duty to do B, and it can be admitted by an externalist. In *Principia Ethica* Moore says, "If I ask whether an action is *really* my duty or *really* expedient, the predicate of which I question the applicability to the action in question is precisely the same. In both cases I am asking, 'Is this event the best on the whole that I can effect?' " Yet, although "duty" and "expedient" have the same conceptual meaning for Moore, he maintains that there is a difference in their use, "duty" being applied to those useful actions "which it is more useful to praise and to enforce by sanctions, since they are actions which there is a temptation to omit." [27] Then "B is A's duty" *means*, "B is the best thing on the whole that A can do," but it *presupposes* that A is tempted not to do it. Perhaps moral judgments only presuppose motivation in a similar sense.

[27] See G. E. Moore, *Principia Ethica* (Cambridge: Cambridge University Press, 1903), pp. 169–70.

VIII

Two other considerations seem to have been regarded as showing that having an obligation entails having a corresponding motivation. One is a conviction that a man cannot have an obligation unless he accepts it as such and "beats responsive and not irresponsive to the claim" in what James calls the "everlasting ruby vaults" of his heart.[28] This is expressed in the following quotation from Falk: ". . . Even the commands of God could only constitute moral obligations for somebody who considered it a *law unto himself* to respect what God bids him to do." [29] Now it does seem in some sense correct to say that a man cannot actually have a moral duty if he does not see and accept it. At the same time, this is an odd thing to say unless we are using "duty" in two senses, for we are saying that A has no duty to do B if he does not recognize that he has a duty to do B. The same double usage occurs in the sentence, "You ought to do what you think you ought to do." The matter can be cleared up by using the distinction, long accepted by externalists, between what one *subjectively* ought to do and what one *objectively* ought to do. The point, then, is that A subjectively ought to do B only if he accepts this as his obligation. It still may be, however, that B would be objectively right for him to do anyway. In fact, when a man thinks that something is his duty, what he thinks is that it is a duty independently of his thinking so (and independently of his wanting to do it); and when he asks what his duty is, he implies that he has a duty that he does not yet recognize, and what he is seeking to know, as it were, is what it would have been his duty to do even if he had not discovered it. Thus

[28] W. James, "The Moral Philosopher and the Moral Life," in *The Will to Believe* (New York: Longmans, Green & Co., 1897), p. 196. James is inconsistent on this point, for he also says that a man has an obligation as soon as someone else makes a demand on him.

[29] "Obligation and Rightness," p. 147.

there is a sense in which one has a moral obligation even if one does not recognize it as such.

It has also been insisted by internalists that the moral will is autonomous, and R. M. Blake believed that this doctrine should be repudiated by externalists as incompatible with the existence of any categorical imperative. Nowell-Smith is especially persistent in asserting such autonomy. ". . . The feature which distinguishes moral obligations from all others is that they are self-imposed. . . ." "The questions 'what shall I do?' and 'what moral principles should I adopt?' must be answered by each man for himself; that at least is part of the connotation of the word 'moral'." [30] In spite of what Blake says, it is hard entirely to reject this "moral protestantism," as Margaret Macdonald has called it,[31] common as it is to Kant, existentialism, and Nowell-Smith. But I am not persuaded that a recognition of autonomy necessarily leads to internalism. In areas outside of ethics we also believe in autonomy, e.g., in our scientific beliefs, and, in "religious protestantism," in our theological beliefs. Yet here the "facts" in which we freely believe or disbelieve are "external" ones—facts which are independent of us but about which we are nevertheless left to make up our own minds. It may then be that obligations are external facts of a similar sort. Certainly intuitionists and naturalists can allow us the same kind of autonomy in ethics that we claim in science and religion, without thereby going over to the enemy. They may hold that what we objectively ought to do is self-imposed only in the sense of being self-discovered or self-recognized, as scientific facts are, and that only what we subjectively ought to do is self-imposed in the more radical manner indicated earlier.

[30] *Ethics*, pp. 210, 320.
[31] Cf. *Philosophical Analysis*, ed. M. Black (Ithaca: Cornell University Press, 1950), p. 220.

IX

However, even if *having* a moral obligation does not always and in every sense depend on the agent's accepting it and feeling motivated to do it, it may nevertheless be maintained that *assenting to* a moral obligation entails a feeling of motivation on his part. This brings us to (7), which is widely insisted on by internalists.[32] It may be put in various ways, but the essential point of it is either (a) that one cannot assent to or be convinced of an obligation of one's own without having some disposition to act accordingly, or (b) that we should regard it as odd or paradoxical if someone were to assent to an obligation without feeling any motivation whatever for fulfilling it. In the first case, there is a direct assertion that a certain sequence of events is not possible; in the second, there is only a claim that we should be puzzled if we observed such a sequence or, rather, do not believe that one can occur.

Now, taken in its first form, (7) does not seem to me to be obviously true. In any case, as we have noticed, it is ambiguous in a way that its proponents do not recognize. Taken as an assertion of a psychological law, it can be admitted by any externalist who does not hold our conative nature to be *totally* depraved.[33] It must then be regarded as asserting a logical truth, if it is to say anything inconsistent with externalism.

[32] See H. J. N. Horsburgh, "The Criteria of Assent to a Moral Rule," *Mind*, N.S. LXIII (1954), 345–58; Hare, *The Language of Morals*, pp. 20, 169.

[33] Cf. Plato, *Symposium*; R. Price, *Review of the Principal Questions of Morals* (Oxford: Clarendon Press, 1948), chap. iii; W. D. Ross, *The Right and the Good*, pp. 157 f. If the doctrine of total depravity does not imply that we have naturally no disposition *whatsoever* to do what is right, but only that such a disposition as we have to do what is right is always overcome by other desires when it comes into conflict with them, except by the grace of God, then even its proponents can accept (7) as a psychological statement.

Here again there are two alternatives. (m) It may be meant that part of what a judgment of obligation *asserts* or *states* is that the agent referred to feels a responsive beat in his heart. Then (7) is identical with (2), and simply to assume it is a *petitio*. (n) The other alternative is that motivation is to be built, not into the content of a moral judgment, but into the process of assenting to it. On this view, it is not "A ought to do B" that logically implies his having some tendency to do B, but "A is convinced that he ought to do B." That is to say, part of what is meant by "assenting to an obligation" is that one feels a responsive stirring.

Most recent internalists, I believe, would prefer this formulation of (7) to that represented by (m). I am not at all sure that (7), so interpreted, is true, but I should like to suggest that an externalist can accept it if it is. An externalist may agree, it seems to me, that we cannot, in the sense in which we use these words in connection with moral judgments, "accept," "recognize," or "be convinced of" an obligation without thereby having at least some motivation to fulfill it. He may hold, for example, that judgments of obligation have a conceptual content of an "external" kind, but add that we do not speak of a man's *assenting* or *sincerely assenting* to them unless he not only apprehends the truth of their conceptual content but is at least to some extent moved to conform to it. He would then admit that it is *logically* possible that one might have a "mere intellectual apprehension," as Field calls it, of their truth, but he would recognize the generally practical function of language (which his opponents have made so much of), especially moral discourse. There is no reason why he cannot change his ways enough to do this; even an intuitionist need not insist that the *actual* use of moral language is merely to report the news of a nonnatural world and is in no way adapted to the interests of the reader. It may be part of the ordinary "grammar" of such words as "assent," when used in connection with ethical judgments, that they are not to be employed except when "mere intellectual apprehension" is accompanied by a responsive beating of the heart. Even in the case of nonethical judgments it has been held that one does not believe unless one is in some sense disposed to act accordingly in appropriate circumstances. But, even if this is not so, it might be argued that because ethical discourse is more particularly concerned to guide human action than is nonethical discourse, such terms as "believe" may be presumed to obey different rules here.

Of course, the internalist may still complain that on his opponent's view it is logically, if not actually, possible to have a "mere intellectual apprehension" of an obligation. But, if the position just described is tenable, then he cannot support his complaint by appealing to the dictum that we cannot really assent to an obligation without having a disposition to respond. And simply to assume that it is not even logically possible to have a "mere intellectual apprehension" of an obligation is a *petitio*.

Consider now (7) in form (b). Here there is an appeal to certain data about our ordinary moral consciousness and its ways of thinking; these data are supposed to show that internalism is true or at least is embedded in moral common sense. Thus Falk has argued that externalism fails to account for such facts as the following:[34] (p) that "we commonly expect that in thinking ourselves obliged we *ipso facto* feel some constraint to do what we think we ought to do"; (q) that, "when we try to convince another that he ought to pay his bills, we expect our argument if accepted to effect some change of heart in him"; (r) that "we should think it odd to receive the answer: 'Yes, I know now *that* and *why* I ought to pay my bills, but I am still without any incentive for doing so.'"

I am not so much concerned to question these facts, though

[34] "Obligation and Rightness," pp. 139–41. Falk also recognizes, however, that externalism "finds some support in common usage" (p. 138).

I do not myself find the answer in (r) entirely odd, as to point out that they do not, as stated, prove obligation and motivation to be *logically* connected. If we have the expectations and feelings of oddity described, this may only mean that we commonly believe that all men are *psychologically* so constituted as to be moved by the recognition that something is right. It need not mean that this is *logically* necessary or even that we believe it to be so. And we have already seen that one may hold rightness to be an external characteristic and yet claim that we are so made as necessarily (causal) to take an interest in it.

Falk's facts may also be explained in another way by the externalist. For, until evidence is given to the contrary, the externalist can argue that the common moral consciousness feels the expectations and oddities mentioned only because it does not distinguish at all clearly or consistently in its thinking between two senses in which one may be obliged, so that it links to the one feelings and thoughts appropriate to the other. This seems to me plausible, for we do frequently fail to see any difference between the two kinds of reasons for action, and often shift from one to the other without noticing.

Still a third explanation is possible. As we have indicated before, when one asks what he ought to do, he is not or at least need not be asking what he already accepts as his duty, but what is his duty although it is not yet accepted as such; and he is not or need not be asking what he has or may have a motive for doing, but what he is morally required to do and may not have any motive for doing until after he sees that it is his duty. But, of course, one would not normally ask the question unless one was concerned about the answer and felt some motivation to do his duty, whatever that might turn out to be. And so, when one concludes that such and such is what he ought to do, he can be expected to feel some motivation to do such and such and even to decide to do it. The whole process of moral question and answer normally takes place in this atmosphere of moral concern. This is all that such facts as those mentioned prove, and this much an externalist may and no doubt should admit, though he may add that it is logically possible that the case should be otherwise. Normally, then, when assent occurs in the course of a moral inquiry, it can be expected to involve commitment. But it does not follow that it is a condition of one's having an obligation to do a certain action that he should have a motive for doing it apart from discovering that it is his duty, nor that discovering it to be his duty logically entails his having a motive for doing it.

It has been argued that, if a man says he believes that he has a duty to do a certain action but feels no conation at all in favor of it, then he does not understand the sentence, "I have a duty," or its use.[35] If by this it is meant that he does not understand what an obligation is, then simply to assert this is to beg the question against the externalist. If it is meant that he does not understand what it is to *assent* to an obligation, the externalist can agree and give the explanation indicated above in our discussion of (7). But it may be that what is intended is that he just does not know in what circumstances to *say*, "I ought to do so and so," and this an externalist may also concede.

X

This brings up a number of points made by internalists, not so much about *having* an obligation or *assenting* to one, as about *uttering* sentences to the effect that one has an obligation or that someone else has—in short, (6). For example, it is said (a) that my uttering a sentence beginning with "I ought" always or normally "expresses" a pro-attitude or de-

[35] E.g., A. Moore, "A Categorical Imperative?" pp. 237 f.; I discuss a similar claim by S. M. Brown, Jr., in "Natural and Inalienable Rights," *Philosophical Review*, LXIV (1955), 222 f.

cision on my part or "contextually implies" one.[36] But this an externalist may grant even if he holds that such a sentence "asserts" an external fact. The sentence, "There are flying saucers," expresses the speaker's belief, but for all that it purports to assert an external fact. Thus, W. D. Ross, who holds that "good" *means* an external characteristic, is "inclined to think" that we *use* or *apply* the term in such a way "that in each case the *judge* has some feeling of approval or interest towards what he calls good." [37] It is also said (b) that my uttering a sentence starting with "You ought" expresses or contextually implies a pro-attitude on my part toward your doing the act specified, as well as one on yours.[38] But Ross could admit this too. If I say, "There is a tidal wave coming up behind you," I "express" a concern about your welfare and "presuppose" that you also have one, but what I assert is still an external fact or purports to be.

In a similar vein internalists contend (c) that it would be absurd, odd, or "logically odd" to say things like: "You ought to do A, but don't"; "I ought to do A, but shall I?"; "I ought to do A, but I shall not." [39] Now these would, perhaps, be unusual uses of language, but are they logically impossible? "There are flying saucers, but I don't believe it" would be an unusual contribution to any serious and sober conversation, but it is not a logically self-contradictory one, since both parts of what is asserted may be true together; the apparent

[36] Cf. Nowell-Smith, *Ethics*, pp. 186 ff., 261; W. S. Sellars, "Obligation and Motivation," in *Readings in Ethical Theory*, p. 516; H. D. Aiken, "Emotive Meanings and Ethical Terms," *Journal of Philosophy*, XLI (1944), 461 ff.; P. B. Rice, *On the Knowledge of Good and Evil* (New York: Random House, 1955), pp. 108 ff., 113, 231 f.

[37] *The Right and the Good*, p. 90.

[38] Nowell-Smith, *Ethics*, p. 199 (the phrase "contextually implies" is owed to Nowell-Smith); Aiken, "Emotive Meanings and Ethical Terms," pp. 461 ff.

[39] Cf. Nowell-Smith, *Ethics*, pp. 146, 152, 178, 261. Note: "I *ought* implies I *shall*" is much stronger than "I *ought* implies I *feel some disposition to*," and an internalist need not hold the former.

conflict is not between parts of what is asserted but between part of what is asserted and one of the presuppositions of asserting the rest.

Logically, as far as I can see, "I should" and "I shall" are distinct, and one can admit that he ought and still not resolve to do. One would not then be very likely to *say*, "I ought but I shall not," for one probably would not be that interested in the morality of what one was doing, but logically the situation would be such as to be describable in those terms. No doubt, as Nowell-Smith and P. B. Rice claim, a firsthand "I ought" does normally express commitment or decision on the speaker's part, for one would not normally go through the process of moral deliberation that concludes with "I ought" if he were not sufficiently devoted to the moral enterprise for this conclusion to coincide with his decision. This does not mean, however, that "I ought" logically entails "I shall"; it may only pragmatically presuppose or contextually imply this.

Nowell-Smith's discussion of "I ought" and "I shall" is interesting in this connection.[40] According to him, "I (morally) ought" expresses a decision, just as "I shall" does, although it is a decision based on rules, and therefore "I ought but shall I?" is logically odd unless "shall I?" is used in a predictive sense. Yet he admits that "I ought" is "also used, not to express a decision, but in the course of making up one's mind before a decision has been reached," and it is this use that interests me. It seems to me that in this use one *could* say, "I ought but shall I?" and one might go on thinking he ought and yet decide not to. Nowell-Smith seeks to avoid this conclusion by turning the "I ought" here into the Voice of Conscience or "self-hortatory 'you ought' "—a neat device but question-begging in this context. The main point, however, is that there is an "I ought" which does not express decision. It is true that this "I ought" is normally replaced by "the

[40] *Ibid.*, pp. 261–63, 267 f.

verdict-giving 'I ought' " *if* desire does not win out over conscience. But desire may win, and then there is a situation which can be described by "I ought, but I shall not," where "shall" is not predictive but decisive, though if one is in this situation one is not likely so to describe it until later, and then in the past tense.

XI

So far our study of the opposition between internalism and externalism in moral philosophy has fallen into two main parts. In the first (sections I through V) we reviewed one family of arguments against externalism and saw that they are not successful, mainly because they can for the most part be answered by distinguishing two senses of "obligation," corresponding to two meanings of, "Why should I?" In the second (sections VI through X) we found that another set of considerations that are relatively independent of this distinction can, in so far as they are valid at all, be met or accepted if certain other distinctions are made—between what we objectively and what we subjectively ought to do; between having an obligation, assenting to an obligation, and saying one has an obligation; between what is stated or logically implied and what is "presupposed" or "implied" in some not strictly logical sense by a moral judgment, and so forth. In short, we have seen that externalism is not refuted by these arguments and considerations and can be maintained if there are not yet other grounds on which it must be given up.

We might now go on to consider corresponding arguments against internalism. It is, however, difficult to find such arguments explicitly set forth in recent literature, and perhaps we may assume that they too would turn out to be inconclusive. The distinction between two senses of "should" and "ought" to which we have appealed, for example, cannot, even if it is valid, be used as an argument to refute internalism, although it disposes of some arguments used in its support.[41] For it is possible to admit this distinction and still maintain a kind of internalism. One might hold, for instance, that moral judgments are expressions of some specifically moral attitude, such as love, sympathy, an internalized sense of social demand, an attitude of impartial spectatorship, and so forth, and regard justifying reasons as reasons calculated to appeal to this attitude, exciting reasons as those that appeal to other attitudes and desires. One would then regard this attitude as conative (unlike Hutcheson's moral sense), and moral judgments as *ipso facto* to some extent motivating. But one would not claim that this attitude is always dominant, and so could admit that I may agree that I ought to do a certain action and yet say, "But I shall not!" In this very important respect one's position, though a form of internalism, would be like externalism.

The main result yielded by our discussion, then, is that the opposition we are studying cannot be resolved, as so many seem to think, by such relatively small-scale logical or semilogical arguments as we have been dealing with. But we have also achieved some clarity about the exact points at issue. The externalist can admit that there is a nonmoral obligation and even a "subjective" moral obligation that logically entails motivation. He can accept any statement that says that having an obligation, assenting to one, or being said to have one causally or *psychologically* involves the existence of a corresponding motivation. He may also agree that assenting to an obligation *logically* entails the existence of motivation for acting accordingly. He may even allow, and perhaps should, that having or being said to have an obligation presupposes in some not strictly logical sense the existence of such motivation. What he must deny, and the internalist assert, is that having objectively a certain moral obligation logically entails having some motivation for fulfilling it, that justifying a judgment of objective moral obligation logically implies establish-

[41] It seems to me also to refute *egoistic* forms of internalism.

ing or producing a motivational buttress, and that it is logically impossible that there should be a state of apprehending a moral obligation of one's own which is not accompanied by such a buttress (even if this "mere intellectual apprehension" is never actual and does not amount to what is called "assenting to" or "acknowledging" an obligation).

Now one may, if sufficiently hardy, choose to defend a form of externalism that does not make any of the concessions just indicated, or a form of internalism that does not incorporate the distinction between two senses of "Why should I?" or between exciting and justifying reasons. Personally, it seems to me that the choice must in practice be between an externalism that makes such concessions and an internalism that recognizes such a distinction. But, in any case, how is the issue to be settled? If arguments of the kind we have been reviewing are inadequate, are we then at an impasse here, too, as so many think we are on other questions? This does not follow. It does follow that neither kind of moral philosophy can be decisively refuted by the other, and that we must give up the quest for certainty in the sense of no longer hoping for such refutations. But it does not follow that nothing can be said for one view as against the other. What does follow is that the whole discussion must consciously move to another level.[42]

This does not mean that it must become even more "meta" than it already is. What this shift involves, and that it is necessary, can best be made clear by taking a look at Falk's best-known paper.[43] Here he first seems to argue very much as he does in the earlier articles already dealt with. But soon it becomes apparent that something different is going on. Falk finds in the controversy between Prichard and his opponents and in moral common sense a tension between two positions, namely,

[42] In "The Naturalistic Fallacy," Mind, N.S. XLVIII (1939), 464–77, I made a similar point about the issue between naturalism and nonnaturalism, but I then had rather simple-minded views about an appeal to "inspection" which was to decide it.

[43] " 'Ought' and Motivation."

"that morality needs some additional psychological sanction" and "that what sanction it requires, it necessarily carries with it." That is, moral philosophy and ordinary moral thinking have been a confused combination of, or alternation between, externalism and internalism. Falk suggests that this situation "has its origin in uncertainties and contradictions in the common use of words like 'ought' or 'duty'; in an unnoticed juxtaposition of meanings each of which entails a different relation to motivation." It is due to the fact that "ought" is used in both an externalist and an internalist sense, which "remain undifferentiated and are imperceptibly juxtaposed and confused," so that "there may be an unnoticed switch from the one use of 'ought' to the other." This is why the questioner's "Why should I be moral?" has been so puzzling. In one sense of "ought" it is "legitimate and in need of some factual answer," in the other it is absurd; and where the two senses are confused "no answer can satisfy," and the way is open for the skeptic to draw his disturbing conclusion.

In other words, Falk, although he is an internalist, is explicitly recognizing the ambiguity we have made so much of —indeed, he goes further and says that one of the senses involved *is* external, a claim we have not made. He uses this ambiguity to explain the rise of our two points of view and their juxtaposition in moral common sense and philosophy. All this I cannot but approve. I have only wanted to add that it is the internalists rather than the externalists who have failed to notice the ambiguity, and that this failure vitiates much of their argument. Falk does not deny this; he simply does not repeat his earlier arguments for internalism, apparently recognizing their insufficiency. Instead, he proceeds to a new line of attack.

Falk contends that we cannot be satisfied, as an externalist would be, with uncovering the confusion and replacing it with an avowed use of "ought" in two senses, one external and one internal, one moral and the other motivational. In fact, he insists that the external use of "ought" cannot be accepted by a mature reflective person who is "aware of a capacity of reasoned choice and intent on using it," because such a person cannot "easily agree to a use of [moral] words for any demand on him that still left him to ask whether he also had a sufficient reason for doing the act." He then argues that one internal use of "ought" bears "at least a sufficient resemblance to what ordinary usage expects of a normative term" for it to qualify as moral.[44] He calls this "the purely formal motivational 'ought.'" To say one ought in this sense is to say he has a reason or motive for acting with regard to which no further question can be asked, or which is compelling no matter what considerations reason may advance, and so is "formally sufficient." This "ought," Falk holds, can be identified with the moral "ought," since it is normative in the sense of influencing "the direction of people's volitional attitudes and actions," it is not simply a function of occurrent wants, and it is categorical, not hypothetical. It is, in fact, confused with the external moral "ought" in ordinary thinking. It *should* be taken as *the* moral "ought" because it must be recognized in any case, and because "in using moral language we mean to denote something that when known, can conclusively serve to direct what we do, and we cannot obey two masters."

Now I am not convinced by what Falk says, all too briefly, even here. He says that "we cannot avowedly use 'moral ought' both for an external and an internal state of affairs, as if a man might have one but not another sort of moral duty in respect of the same act." Yet he has not shown that we ever do use the *moral* "ought" for an internal state of affairs, but at most that we ought to. Besides, in the distinction between a subjective and an objective "ought" it seems to be possible to use even "morally ought" in two senses, one more internal and one more external, without thereby having to

[44] In "Morals without Faith," Falk distinguished four senses of "should" or "ought," one "moral" but all "internal."

serve two masters. Moreover, it does not appear that his substitute will do as the moral "ought." As far as I can see, an
act may be morally wrong even though I am impelled to do
it after full reflection. What one is impelled to do even after
reason has done its best is still dependent on the vagaries of
one's particular conative disposition, and I see no reason for
assuming that it will always coincide with what is in fact right
or regarded as right. As for Falk's assertion that "in using
moral language we mean to denote something that when
known, can conclusively serve to direct what we do"—this is
ambiguous. It may mean that moral judgments are intended
to serve as conclusive *guides* or that they are meant to serve
as conclusive *goads*. In the first case Falk is clearly right, but
an externalist can agree. In the second he is either forgetting
his own admission that there is an external use of "ought" in
ordinary discourse or begging the question. His further claim
that a reflective person cannot accept as a moral duty anything which he does not have a "formally sufficient" motive
for doing seems to me to beg the question as it stands.

What interests me here about Falk's paper, however, is the
fact that he has moved the controversy to another level, a less
merely logical and larger scale level. The issue, he says in conclusion, is not settled merely by distinguishing "between
normative facts of different kinds, confusedly referred to by
the same name"; ultimately what is necessary is "clarity and
decision about what fact would most nearly correspond to our
intentions in the use of moral language and which words like
'ought' and 'duty' should be made to denote." This is the
problem as it shapes itself at the end of our study. Externalism
versus internalism, yes, but on a macroscopic rather than a
microscopic plane. These are not small positions that may be
decisively established or taken in a brief action recorded in a
page or two. They are whole theories of "our intentions in the
use of moral language," past, present, and future.

To see this let us glance at the internalist case, as it must be made if the above discussion has been correct. Central in it must be the contention that externalism leaves a gap between perceived obligation and motivation. Now, we have seen that externalism does not *logically* entail the existence of a *psychological* gap here. By itself it entails only that it is logically possible that one should in some sense perceive (though perhaps without giving a full-fledged *assent*) that one has an obligation and yet have no disposition to fulfill it. That is, the argument that externalism logically involves a gap does not come off; externalism implies only that there is a logical gap or that it is logically possible there is a psychological gap, and it is simply begging the question to begin with the opposite premise. But instead of reasoning in this way, as in effect the writers we have dealt with do, the internalist may and should elaborate his case as follows.

1. Externalism does not by itself logically imply that there may (psychologically) be a gap between perceived obligation and motivation, but it implies that such a gap is logically possible. This is true in the qualified sense just indicated.

2. An externalist may claim that there is in fact no gap—that actually there is always some possibly adequate motivation for doing what one perceives to be right—and he may offer various psychological theories in his support. He may hold that a "mere intellectual apprehension" of one's duty is itself moving, that there is in human nature a desire to do what is right, that the sentiment of benevolence is always on hand to support the call of duty, and so forth. But all such theories are false; there is no external fact which the externalist may plausibly identify with obligation which is also such that its apprehension is always, let alone by a psychological necessity, accompanied by a responsive beating of the heart. Therefore, there is in fact a psychological gap between obligation and motivation if any form of externalism is true, in the sense that then one actually might perceive an obligation and have no corresponding motivation.

3. At this point the internalist may argue either that there is in fact no psychological gap, that the existence of such a gap is intolerable from the point of view of morality, or that our moral common sense does not believe there is such a gap, concluding that externalism is false or inconsistent with common sense.

Such a line of reasoning involves first establishing (2), and this requires a full-scale psychological inquiry, which is more than internalists have yet gone in for. Suppose that it is established. All that follows is that, if externalism is true, human beings may sometimes lack all motivation to do what they apprehend as right. One who is willing to admit this need follow the argument no farther. This brings us to (3). To argue here that there is no gap is to make a factual, psychological claim, the establishing of which again calls for an empirical inquiry, one as difficult to handle as the question whether Socrates was correct in believing that we always do what we think is right. It is hard to see how it could be carried out without taking some position with respect to the definition of obligation, assenting, and so forth, and it is just this that constitutes our problem. In any case, the record of human conduct is not such as to make it obvious that human beings always do have some tendency to do what they regard as their duty. The contention that our common moral consciousness supposes that there can be no gap will be met by conflicting evidence, as Falk admits, and, in any event, one may reply that common sense may be mistaken, thus opening the whole question again. If the contention is only that it is a rule of ordinary moral discourse that a person shall not be *said* to have an obligation unless there is or may be presumed to be in him some disposition to respond favorably, then, as we have seen, the externalist may admit it, but he may also contest it or argue for a change in the rules.

It seems to me, therefore, that in the end the internalist must argue, as Falk does, not only that externalism involves a gap between obligation and motivation, but that such a gap cannot be tolerated, given morality's task of guiding human conduct autonomously. Then, however, the externalist will counter by pointing out that internalism also entails a danger to morality. Externalism, he will say, in seeking to keep the obligation to act in certain ways independent of the vagaries of individual motivation, runs the risk that motivation may not always be present, let alone adequate, but internalism, in insisting on building in motivation, runs the corresponding risk of having to trim obligation to the size of individual motives.

Here the true character of the opposition appears. Each theory has strengths and weaknesses, and deciding between them involves determining their relative total values as accounts of morality. But such a determination calls for a very broad inquiry. It cannot be based on individual preference. We must achieve "clarity and decision" about the nature and function of morality, of moral discourse, and of moral theory, and this requires not only small-scale analytical inquiries but also studies in the history of ethics and morality, in the relation of morality to society and of society to the individual, as well as in epistemology and in the psychology of human motivation.[45]

[45] Suggestions of such "macroscopic" considerations as I describe here may be found in Nowell-Smith, *Ethics*, chap. i and p. 267; C. L. Stevenson, "The Emotive Conception of Ethics and Its Cognitive Implications," *Philosophical Review*, L (1950), 294 f.; H. D. Aiken, "A Pluralistic Analysis of the Ethical 'Ought' " and "The Authority of Moral Judgments"; and in two less technical works: W. T. Stace, *The Destiny of Western Man* (New York: Reynal & Hitchcock, 1942), and Erich Fromm, *Man for Himself* (New York: Rinehart & Co., 1947). In fact, Field, *Moral Theory*, pp. 51, 52, 56 f., broaches the line of argument sketched in this last section, but in a very incomplete way. Such a macroscopic line of reasoning must also be in W. S. Sellars' mind in "Obligation and Motivation," note 36, as a support for his identification of moral obligation with a certain kind of motivation, though he appears to expound only this conclusion without the supporting argumentation.

The battle, if war there be, cannot be contained; its field is the whole human world, and a grand strategy with a total commitment of forces is demanded of each of its participants. What else could a philosopher expect?

H. L. A. HART

Legal and Moral Obligation

Moral philosophers in both England and America have long spoken and written as if the phenomenon under investigation was primarily, if not exclusively, moral *obligation* or moral *duty*; very few have questioned the suitability of the expressions "obligation" and "duty" to describe the principal subject of their study. Yet, as their examples show, these philosophers have been very much concerned with such actions as the gratuitous infliction of pain on children or animals, the killing of human beings, the heartless abandonment of friends, lying and other forms of deception. Something more, I hope, than a blind wish to adhere to our common speech prompts the protest that it is absurd to speak of having a moral *duty* not to kill another human being, or an *obligation* not to torture a child. Surely when we are moved by moral repugnance and shrink from some squalid action the situation is ill-conveyed by saying that here we are acknowledging a *duty*; and surely it is at least misleading to say that we have acknowledged (or recognized) an *obligation* when in difficult circumstances, not provided for by anything that could reasonably be called a rule, we think out the consequences of alternative lines of conduct and decide what on the whole is best to do.

The point of such a protest is not, or at any rate not merely, that "duty" or "obligation" are too weak, too feeble in condemnatory force, for the blacker moral offenses. "Obligation" and "duty" are not inappropriate here because they are reserved for the relatively minor matters on a single moral scale to which belong also more serious elements (moral crimes). The point, rather, is that they do not belong to the same scale and the extension of these terms to the whole field of morality blinds us to its variety and complexity.

Two considerations might perhaps alert us to this fact. The first is that among the examples used by moral philosophers there are certainly some where the expressions "obligation" and "duty" sit quite happily. Moral obligations do arise from promises, from the position of parent, and there may be a moral obligation to obey the law. So, too, moral duties do spring from positions of trust like that of a confidential servant, or from recognized positions or roles in a social group such as that of being a host or a neighbor, a husband or a father. Such cases where the terminology of obligation and duty is so obviously appropriate have, I think, discernible common or related features, and these contrast with the kind of thing at stake when we insist that we ought not to inflict gratuitous pain. What tends to obscure the difference is that "ought" (and in some contexts both "must" and "should") may be used in urging others to abstain both from breaking their promises and from torturing children, and in moral criticism of these offenses when committed. Yet this is no better ground for the identification of what are disparate, though of course related, segments of morality than is the fact that, given appropriate contexts, "ought," "must," and "should" may be used when it is patent that nothing moral is at stake. You ought to, you should, you must change your wet clothes.

Second, and more important, there is a whole world where duties and obligations are really at home. This is the legal world: for here both expressions are almost always appropriate for whatever the rules of an actually existing legal system forbid. If a statute forbids cruelty to children or animals, then we have a legal duty to forbear from such cruelty. In speaking of the legal obligation to do what we have bound ourselves by contract to do, we make no more felicitous use of the word "obligation" than when we speak of the legal obligation to keep off other people's land, or to refrain from assaulting or libeling them; but in ordinary nonlegal discourse and in morals it is different. So in the succeeding sections of this paper I propose first to inquire into the character of legal obligation and then to determine why in referring to certain moral situations we naturally make use of the legally colored concepts of obligation and duty.

I

It may perhaps help with the understanding of legal obligation and duty if we begin, not with an onslaught on definition, but by noting some of the remarkable things that can, in any developed legal system, be done about them, and hence be said about them. First and foremost, it is the case (and perhaps more obviously true of obligations than of many other features of a legal system) that legal obligations are very often (though not always) human artifacts in the sense that they may be deliberately created by the appropriate action of human beings and subjected to various modes of change and manipulation. Their status as obligations may be independent of their content for we not only may *have* legal duties and obligations, but we may *create*, or *impose* them (e.g., by legislation), or *incur* or *assume* them (e.g., by making contracts). They may be *varied* and *modified* and *extinguished*; and persons may (notably where obligations are created by contract) be *released* from them.

Of course, in any developed legal system, not only obligations or duties but other legal entities (rights, powers, immunities, and disabilities) may be similarly created, modified, or extinguished; and rights may be transferred, e.g., when property is alienated upon a sale. The most prominent and important example of the deliberate *creation* of legal duties and obligations is the creation of a legal obligation by legislative enactment. In any modern society legislation is a very complex operation. The legislative process involves not only the cooperation of numerous persons qualified under existing legal rules to take part, but also their compliance with a complex procedure determined by legal rules, which exist and are accepted as governing the process. Normally, the crucial step is a vote for or against a legislative proposal usually presented in written form. Given such circumstances, the upshot of the vote and of certain subsequent formalities (assent by the Queen, or signature by the President, or lapse of a certain time without notice of disapproval) is that a law is *made* or *enacted*, introducing, say, two years of military service for all males between the ages of twenty-one and thirty-five, or prohibiting the sale of intoxicating liquors. In this manner legislators create obligations and impose them on others (and on themselves in their personal capacity) who are thenceforth legally bound to do or forbear doing certain things. Subordinate authorities may also by enactment be given a derivative legal *power* to create further obligations and duties within a certain area.

It is perhaps useful to compare and contrast these legislative operations with those operations whereby a person also creates obligations but imposes them, not on others, but only upon himself. The most notable example of this is, of course, the bilateral or consensual contract which is the legal analogue of the promise where, e.g., one man binds himself to deliver a ton of bricks to another by a certain date in consideration of the other's binding himself to pay £100 for them. But there are other forms of self-imposition of obligation: both in the

English and in the American systems a person may declare himself a trustee of property perhaps for persons yet unborn, and immediately thereupon is under obligation or duty not to deal with it in certain ways which were open to him up to that point.

How are the creation, imposition, modification, and extinction of obligations and other operations on other legal entities such as rights possible? How can such things be done? This Kantian-sounding question can only be answered by describing in detail how in fact they are done. The lawyer, so used to this kind of thing, would reply in his own terminology, "These things can be done because the law confers *powers* upon persons to do these things: they do them in the exercise of legal powers." But the philosopher may well inquire: What are these powers? What is it for a law to confer a power and for someone to exercise such a power? "Power" here does not mean capacity to bring about observable physical change, and certainly to some these operations have appeared a sort of legal (and moral) alchemy, not susceptible of any explanation. Hagerström,[1] faced with the difficulties of analyzing the simplest one of such operations, namely, the transfer of ownership, concluded that the character of all such operations could only be elucidated by reference to a widespread belief in the magical powers of words to bring about changes in a supra-sensible world of legal rights and duties. He developed his theories mainly in relation to Roman law, starting from the acute observation that the crucial words used by the purchaser in the *mancipatio*, the Roman formal transfer of property ("I say this slave is mine according to the law"), could not be intended as a statement of ordinary fact since the words, if treated as a statement, would be false at the time

[1] See Axel Hagerström, *Inquiry into the Nature of Law and Morals*, ed. Karl Olivecrona, trans. C. D. Broad (Stockholm: Almqvist & Wiksell, 1953), and the present writer's review in *Philosophy*, XXX (1955), 369–73.

they were spoken, for the ownership did not "pass" to the purchaser till later.

This certainly was a flash of insight, but Hagerström's approach suffered badly from the failure to notice that the theory that the creation, transfer, or modification of obligations and rights was "magical" had just as much (so just as little) force in relation to the central operative words used in the enactment of a modern statute imposing obligations, or the operative words (words of grant) in a private document such as conveyance or will. The modern legislative formulas ("Now it is hereby enacted") and the operative words ("X hereby conveys unto Y," "I hereby bequeath to B") taken as statements of facts are also false, for the "acts," "deeds," or "instruments" in which they appear do not "take effect" until further formalities (signing, sealing, witnessing, delivery, and so forth) are completed or often until some later event happens, such as the testator's death in the case of a will.

So Hagerström leaves us with the residual problem: How can words have legal effects, and what are the effects that they have? Our concern is only with a special part of his question: How can words create legal obligations, and what are the legal obligations they create? But even this necessarily involves consideration of the foundation of any legal system, and of part of what is involved in the assertion that a legal system exists; for any answer that stops short of this will leave the original problem on our hands. Thus we might, indeed, we must, begin by saying that, if words are to be used to create legal obligations, rules of the system must exist providing that if they are used (by the appropriate persons in the appropriate circumstances) these persons designated by these words shall be legally bound or have a legal obligation to do or to abstain from certain actions. It is easy to see that both behind the words used by a municipal corporation enacting a bylaw imposing an obligation on occupiers of land to drain or to fence it in from the highway, and behind the words used in a lease

under which the tenant has an obligation to pay rent, there
must be rules of the system providing that if certain words
are used in this way then the occupiers of land in the one
case and the tenant in the other case shall have these obligations. But what does it mean to say of those rules that they
exist and that they provide that persons shall have such obligations? In the case of subordinate rules of the system, such
as the statutes conferring legislative powers on a municipal
corporation, the assertion that the rules exist means that they
belong to a class of rules marked off as valid rules of the particular system by criteria specified in the fundamental rules of
the system, such as the English rule that what the Queen in
Parliament enacts is law, or in the United States the rule of
the Constitution that (subject to certain restrictions) what
Congress enacts is law in certain fields. But to say of these
fundamental rules (which provide and specify the legislative
competence of the legislative authority) that they *exist* is to
say something different. "Exist" here cannot mean "valid,
given the system's criteria of validity" as, roughly, it does in
the case of subordinate rule of the system. In this case "exists"
must refer to the *actual practice* of the particular social group
whose legal system is under consideration. Even in the case
of the simplest imaginable legal system where a monarch has
unrestricted legislative authority to enact law imposing legal
obligations by pronouncing or writing down what he requires
to be done, the actual practice of the group presupposed by
the assertion that he has this authority is complex and not
shortly describable. It was too shortly described by Austin [2]
as a general habit of obedience to a person or persons not in
a like habit of obedience to others. Kelsen,[3] seeing the in-

[2] See John Austin, *The Province of Jurisprudence Determined*, ed.
H. L. A. Hart (London: Weidenfeld & Nicolson, 1954), Lecture VI,
pp. 198–205.

[3] See Hans Kelsen, *General Theory of Law and State* (Cambridge,
Mass.: Harvard University Press, 1949): ". . . a juristic hypothesis—
that is, a basic norm, to be established by a logical analysis of actual

adequacies of this formulation, divorced the "basic norm" of a legal system from any actual practice by misleadingly characterizing it as a fundamental "hypothesis" or "postulate" made by the jurist examining the system. The inadequacies of both these extremes have led others to insist that what is at the root of every legal system is a general recognition of a *moral* obligation to obey the law so that there is a necessary [4] or analytic connection and not merely an empirical one between the statement that a legal system exists and the statement that most of the population recognizes a moral obligation to obey the law.

To steer between these aberrations of juristic theory it is necessary first to see why "habit" and "obedience" are not enough to characterize the situation in which we say legal obligations are created by legislation. If members of a group merely have a *habit* of obeying an individual, X, who threatens them and is able to harm them in the event of disobedience, this situation might be described by saying they are *obliged* or *compelled* to obey him or to do what he says, but not by saying that they have or recognize an *obligation* to do what

---

juristic thinking" (p. xv); "The basic norm of a legal order is the postulated ultimate rule according to which the norms of this order are established and annulled, receive and lose their validity" (p. 113); "That the basic norm really exists in the juristic consciousness is the result of a simple analysis of actual juristic statements" (p. 116).

[4] See, for example, A. L. Goodhart, *English Law and the Moral Law* (London: Stevens & Sons, 1953): "By blandly suggesting that this basic norm must be 'presupposed to be binding' Kelsen avoids the most important problem in legal philosophy" (p. 18); "If . . . we regard the law as a rule which is recognised as obligatory then the element of force becomes of minor importance. We then realise that the obligatory nature of these rules is based on other grounds, and that one of the most important of these is that of moral law. It is for this reason that the moral sense is one of the dominant forces not only in establishing the efficacy of law, but also in its very existence. The jurist cannot ignore the moral law as irrelevant to his subject because if he does so then he will be ignoring one of the grounds on which the basic idea of obligation is based" (p. 28).

X says. If we are to speak of their having or recognizing an obligation to do what X says, their attitude to X's words must be more than habitual obedience. The minimum required in *addition* to general obedience, if we are to speak of the group's recognizing or having a legal obligation to do something specified by X, is (1) that X's words should generally be accepted as constituting a standard of behavior so that deviations from it (unlike the mere failure to follow a mere habit current in the society, such as that of drinking tea or coffee) are treated as occasions for criticism of various sorts; (2) that references to X's words are generally made as *reasons* for doing or having done what X says, as supporting *demands* that others should do what he says, and as rendering at least permissible the application of coercive repressive measures to persons who deviate from the standard constituted by X's words.

How many of the social group (subjects or officials) must do these things, how continuously, and how long to constitute "general" obedience and "general" use of X's words in this way admits of no determinate answer, just as we are not called on to say exactly how old a man must be to be middle-aged. But in any social group where obligations are created by legislation, and the expressions "I have a legal obligation to do this" and "He has a legal obligation to do that" have their present force, there must be a social practice at least as complex as I have described and not merely habitual obedience on the part of the members of the group. Anyone who uses such forms of expression as "I (you) have an obligation to" implies that his own attitude to the legislator's words is that described, for these statements of obligation are used to draw conclusions from legal rules on the footing that the rules are authoritative for the speaker. One who repudiated the authority altogether might of course recognize that he would be made to suffer if he disobeyed the rules, but the natural expression for this point of view would be not "I (you) have an obligation to" but "I am (you are) obliged to" or "under this system I (you) will suffer if I (you) do not."

The foregoing perhaps sufficiently shows the inadequacies of the characterization of the root of a legal system in terms of a *habit* of obedience. Kelsen was right in insisting that there must be more than habits or regularities of behavior in the narrow sense of regularly doing what the authority says. Yet his conception of the basic norm as a rule, "hypothesis," or "axiom," the "validity" of which is "assumed" or "postulated" [5] brings in a set of quite inappropriate quasi-mathematical expressions that we might indeed adopt if those were the only alternatives to describing the relevant facts in terms of "habits of obedience." But there is a third alternative, and this is to describe the relevant facts in terms not of habits but of the rules actually accepted by a social group. The question whether a group does accept a given rule is different in the ways already indicated from the question whether it habitually obeys a person, though the two questions are alike in that both are questions of fact and Austin is to be preferred to Kelsen for seeing that a statement of fact and not an "assumption of validity" is presupposed in any statement that someone has a legal obligation. If a group of persons behaves in the way we have distinguished as accepting what a legislator says as constituting a standard of behavior, then they accept the rule that he is to be obeyed, and then the rule that his word is law exists. The rule that what the Queen in Parliament enacts is law exists in this way. Once such a rule is thus found to exist in the actual practice of a group, it is absurd to speak of it as a *valid* rule, equally absurd to speak of it as *invalid* or of *assuming* or *postulating* its *validity*. We

[5] See Kelsen, *General Theory of Law and State*, as cited above and as follows: "The validity of this first constitution is the last presupposition, the final postulate, upon which the validity of all the norms of our legal order depends" (p. 115); "The basic norm is an indispensable assumption because, without it, the normative character of the basic historical event could not be established" (p. 396).

might as well speak of postulating or assuming the validity of an actually existing social rule that we take hats off on entering a house. Of course we can raise a number of different questions about such rules, e.g., whether it is a good or desirable thing that members of a group should accept them or have a moral obligation to go on with them, but it is most confusing to discuss this question in terms of "validity."

The third misconception, namely, that if a legal system exists there must (logically) be a general recognition of a *moral* obligation to obey the law, is an excessive reaction to Kelsen's geometrical characterization of the basic norm. Of course it is probably true that unless a majority voluntarily cooperated in obeying the rules of a coercive legal system it could not endure; it may even be true that unless a great number conceived themselves and others morally bound to obey, the system might be quite unstable. But this is insufficient to demonstrate the alleged *logical* connection between "There is a legal system in England" and "In England there is a general recognition of a moral obligation to obey the law," though the first of these is certainly true and the second is probably true. Equally irrelevant to the precise point are the undoubted facts that the development of the law by courts and legislature has been powerfully influenced by the moral convictions of the population and always will be. This does not show that no legal system exists unless obedience is motivated by a conviction that there is a moral obligation to obey. The assertion that there is a legal system in England (or anywhere else) does entail that there is in fact general acceptance of a fundamental rule such as the rule that what the Queen in Parliament enacts is law, though its form may be far more complex than this: general acceptance of such a rule does consist in more than habitual obedience for it includes the further use of, and attitude to, the enacted law which I have described. But both this general obedience and the further use of and attitudes to the law may be motivated by fear, inertia, admiration of tradition, or long-sighted calculation of selfish interests as well as by recognition of moral obligation. As long as the general complex practice is there, this is enough to answer affirmatively the inquiry whether a legal system exists. The question of what motivates the practice, though important, is an independent inquiry.

Once the complex social practice is established whereby a person's words are accepted as constituting a standard of behavior to the group, the legislative authority thereby constituted need not (though it may) be limited to the simple case of direct creation of obligation by legislation enjoining or forbidding specific actions or classes of action. The legislator may have authority to enact further rules conferring authority on others similar to his own for the regulation of limited areas of conduct (subordinate legislation) or rules empowering private individuals to create obligations for themselves, e.g., by contract. But the obligations created in those derivative ways under enacted rules owe their status as obligations ultimately to the underlying practice of the social group in accepting the legislative enactments as constituting standards of behavior and can be understood only if we understand the simple fundamental case of the creation of obligation by direct enactment and its dependence on the complex social practice that constitutes this basic authority.

We now can consider shortly those cases where legal obligations are not *created* at all but arise directly not under rules that have been deliberately introduced by legislation but under customary rules, and also those obligations that are created by the exercise of power conferred by such customary rules. Hitherto we have concentrated attention on those legal obligations that are brought into existence by deliberate legislation in order to demonstrate certain important features; it is, however, true that in most legal systems many rules under which obligations arise are not deliberately created but are

customary in origin. "Custom" is usually a subordinate criterion of validity in modern legal systems in the sense that
such customary rules may be deprived of their validity by
legislative enactment while the converse in most cases is not
true; but there is no *logical* reason (though every practical
reason) why a legal system should not have as its sole criterion
of validity the rule that only those rules are valid which represent the customary long-established practice of the group in
certain matters or the practice of some subgroup. In such
cases authority is not attributed to the holder of any office
and obligations are not conceived as created by deliberate acts
but as owing their status to the fact of traditional practice:
this practice is taken as the standard. Sometimes even the
degree of generalization involved in the recognition of "custom" as a general criterion of validity may not be achieved.
There may be no recognition of any general principle as rendering actions legally obligatory but only a discrete set of rules
may exist, which means that the social group simply accepts
certain distinct types of conduct as standards of behavior and
for the criterion of behavior in the way described. This plainly
would be near the vanishing point of legal *system*.

It remains only to draw attention to the fact that, even
where legal rules are customary, powers to create obligations
may arise under such rules. The power to create obligations
by simple contract in many Anglo-American jurisdictions
arises under common law rules that were not introduced by
deliberate legislation, but are conceived of as representing
the long-established customary practice of the courts. Of
course where a legal system exists containing among its criteria
of validity a rule of precedent, i.e., that those rules are valid
which are extracted from past cases by loosely defined rules
of interpretation, the line between those rules that owe their
validity to an authority's deliberate act and those that do not
becomes blurred though not (as some Realists have argued)
nonexistent.

II

We have yet to discuss in detail what most people would regard as *the* salient feature of an obligation and to some extent of duties: this is the important connection between obligation and coercion or compulsion. If we have an obligation to do something there is some sense in which we are bound to do it, and where we are bound there is some sense in which we are or may be compelled to do it. To probe these notions it is important to distinguish three things: (1) being physically compelled to do something, (2) being obliged to do something, (3) having an obligation to do something. The difficulty of the topic is that of stating without exaggeration the relation between the third member of this trio and the others, and Austin, who made in the introductory sections of *The Province of Jurisprudence Determined* the most painstaking effort to understand the notion of obligation, did fatally exaggerate this relation. He perceived correctly that when a man is dragged to prison, and so in some sense compelled to enter it, this is not a case of having an obligation or duty to go there. But, though he avoided this mistake, Austin defined obligation and duty in terms of the sanction or evil which one who commands (signifies his desire to another that he should do something) threatens to inflict in the event of disobedience.[6] To have a duty or an obligation, according

[6] See Austin, *The Province of Jurisprudence Determined*: "Being liable to evil from you if I comply not with a wish which you signify, I am *bound* or *obliged* by your command, or I lie under a *duty* to obey it" (p. 14); ". . . wherever a duty lies, a command has been signified; and whenever a command is signified, a duty is imposed" (p. 14); "The evil which will probably be incurred in case a command be disobeyed or (to use an equivalent expression) in case a duty be broken, is frequently called a *sanction*, or an *enforcement of obedience*. Or (varying the phrase) the command or duty is said to be *sanctioned* or *enforced* by the chance of incurring the evil" (p. 15); "When I am talking *directly* of the chance of incurring the evil, or (changing the expression) of the liability or obnoxiousness to the evil, I employ the term *duty*, or the term *obligation* . . ." (p. 18).

to Austin, is to be liable or obnoxious to an evil so threatened
where "liable" or "obnoxious" means "likely to incur." The
most obvious defect of this definition is that it would be
satisfied by the case of a gunman's ordering me to hand over
my purse at the point of a gun, where we would *not* say, "I
had an obligation to hand over my purse"; what encourages
the mistake is that we *would* say in such a case, "I was *obliged*
to hand over my purse." So at first sight Austin's account
looks like a fairly accurate definition of "being obliged" to do
something and a very poor definition of "having an obligation" to do something. But we must take into account Austin's
additions to and refinements upon his starting point. His account of specifically *legal* obligation differs from the primitive
example of the gunman in a number of respects. Instead of
the gunman, we have the sovereign defined as the person or
persons whom the bulk of society generally obey, and who
is himself not in a like habit of obedience to anyone else;
further, commands of the sovereign are to follow "general" [7]
courses of conduct and are addressed usually to numbers of
persons. Apart from these qualifications for the special case of
legal obligation, Austin also insists that his definition would
be satisfied even if the chance of incurring the threatened
evil was very small, and the evil itself was very small: "the
slightest chance of the slightest evil" is enough to constitute
obligation or duty.[8] Lastly, Austin, albeit with hesitation, suggests that if a person has an obligation or duty he must have
the threatened evil "in prospect," i.e., fear it,[9] though certainly this psychological element is little stressed.

[7] *Ibid.*: "Now where it obliges *generally* to acts or forbearances of a
class, a command is a law or rule" (p. 19).

[8] *Ibid.*: "But where there is the smallest chance of incurring the
smallest evil, the expression of a wish amounts to a command, and,
therefore, imposes a duty. The sanction, if you will, is feeble or insufficient; but still there *is* a sanction, and, therefore, a duty and a command" (p. 16).

[9] *Ibid.*: "If, in spite of that evil in prospect, I comply not with the

Unfortunately these additions and refinements cause Austin's analysis to fall between two stools. It ceases to be a plausible analysis of "being obliged" to do something and remains an inadequate analysis of "having an obligation." To see precisely where it fails we must concede something which may be disputed: Austin would not allow any system of rules to count as a legal system unless its rules provided for the infliction of evil in the case of disobedience. We may for the purpose of the argument concede this as a part of the definition of "legal," though it was deduced by Austin from propositions that we might wish to reject: he thought laws were commands, and he thought commands were significations of desire by one who had the intention and some ability to inflict some evil in the event of disobedience. But, even if we concede the analytical connection between the notion of a legal system and that of a sanction in the form of evil or harm, the definition of having an obligation in terms of the *chance* of incurring the threatened evil, and of the individual's having this evil in prospect, leads to absurdities.

We may deal first with the psychological element (prospect of evil), which Austin only very uncertainly uses. The statement that a thief has a legal obligation not to take the purse is not a psychological statement about him. He may have no fear at all of the threatened evil, and yet his obligation remains. If he is deterred by fear we may say, rather oddly, that he was obliged to leave it alone. Second, the statement that a person has an obligation on a particular occasion is quite independent of any assessment of the chances of his incurring the evil though these may be very important in considering where he could be said to be obliged to do something

---

wish which you signify, I am said to disobey your command, or to violate the duty which it imposes" (p. 14); ". . . *superiority* signifies *might*: the power of affecting others with evil or pain, and of forcing them, through fear of that evil, to fashion their conduct to one's wishes" (p. 24).

that he did on a particular occasion. There is no contradiction or even oddity in saying, "It's your duty to report for military service, but, since you're living in Monte Carlo and there's no extradition treaty, there's not the slightest chance of their getting you."

Third, there is something quite ludicrous in Austin's first stressing the importance of the threatened evil and then reducing it to "the slightest chance of the slightest evil." This ruins his analysis as an analysis even of being obliged to do something. Only where a choice is made less eligible by some substantial disadvantage do we speak of being obliged.

The most general criticism of Austin's analysis of obligation is that his inadequate notions of chance of incurring evil, prospect of threatened evil, are misleading because they obscure a central element, and this is simply the existence of rules of the appropriate kind. The most charitable view of Austin's talk of the chances of incurring evil is to regard it as expressing in inappropriate predictive terminology the following two facts: (1) if a legal system is to exist under which obligations are created there must at its root be the complex social practice we have already described; (2) the system must contain rules providing for the application of sanctions in the event of disobedience though not all rules need have sanctions "annexed" to them. Without the notion of a system of rules resting on that complex social practice, the difference between "obliging" and "imposing or creating an obligation" cannot be made clear.

Hence the important connection between the concept of coercion and obligation cannot be clearly stated in Austinian terms with its impoverished vocabulary of habit and its inadequate analysis of a command in terms of the expression of a wish that people should act in certain ways made by one who intends and has some power to visit disobedience with some evil. The coercion in question may indeed take the form of the infliction of evil as it does in the case of a municipal legal system, but if it does the application of the evil must be something for which the rules of the system itself provide. However clear the actual power of a legislator was to visit certain conduct with pains, his threat and even use of force to coerce people to obey him would not constitute an obligation unless these were provided for by means of the appropriate legislative forms. At the most people would be obliged to do what he said. So the essential element of coercion is not the fact (the chance or the prospect) that evil will follow disobedience, but there should be an existing system of rules conferring authority on persons to prohibit behavior and to visit breaches of the prohibition with the appropriate coercive, repressive, or punitory techniques of the system.

Some qualification though not abandonment must be made of this last point. In all municipal legal systems there are some cases where there is no provision for sanctions in the event of a breach of a rule. Though perhaps no logical vice or infinite regress would attach to a self-referring rule that all officials should exact sanctions for all offenses including any breach of this rule itself, it is quite common for legal rules to require officials to do certain things and for the system to provide no sanction in the case of their breach. This is for example the case with the obligation imposed by the United States Constitution on the President to take care for the due execution of the laws. Yet we do not hesitate to refer to such cases as cases of official duty or obligation. They show that even within a legal system the complex features that characterize the standard case of obligation may come apart. This is reflected in juristic terminology, such as that of "duties of imperfect obligation," which the Romans invented for just such cases; and it helps to generate part of the skeptical doubts whether international law is "really" law or better classified as a branch of morality.

III

Within the vaguely bounded field of morality, there is certainly a sector (no doubt also vaguely bounded) in which we make use of a concept characterized by three salient features distinctive of the concept of a legal obligation. These features I shall refer to by terms that I hope will be found self-explanatory: (1) dependence on the actual practice of a social group, (2) possible independence of content, and (3) coercion. Outside philosophy, the expressions "obligation" and "duty" are used mainly for the appraisal or criticism of conduct by standards that have these three features and are not used indifferently for all forms of moral judgment. But certainly even nonphilosophical usage sometimes extends beyond this, and my concern is not to legislate in favor of a more restricted use of these expressions but only to determine the differences between different sorts of moral phenomena obscured by this extension. This is worth doing for perhaps two reasons: first, there is undoubtedly a standing temptation in philosophy to assimilate all types of moral judgment to a single type; second, we can best understand other areas of morality if we *first* focus clearly on the three salient features of obligation as they appear in the actual morality of a social group. To characterize morality (as, e.g., R. M. Hare does in his illuminating book, *The Language of Morals* [10]) as *primarily* a matter of the application to conduct of those ultimate principles which the individual accepts or to which he commits himself for the conduct of his life seems to me an excessively Protestant approach. Important as this aspect or kind of moral judgment is, we need to understand it as a development from the primary phenomenon of the morality of a social group.

In suggesting that we distinguish one type of moral judgment from another, I do not in the least wish to deny that

[10] R. M. Hare, *The Language of Morals* (Oxford: Clarendon Press, 1952).

the conduct that they require may often be identical. It is often the case that one and the same particular action is required by different moral principles. If I promise to look after and protect a neighbor's child I have an obligation to do this which arises from my promise; but I may also think it inconsistent with my moral principles to permit unnecessary suffering of this as of any other child though I should not naturally phrase my recognition of this latter principle in terms of recognizing an obligation. Here is one way in which different principles of moral conduct overlap. But they may also coincide in a different and more important way. It may be that the social group in which we live and accept the institution of a promise as breeding obligations also endorses the different and wider principle that it is wrong to inflict gratuitous suffering. Even here, so long as we think that the force of this wider principle does not depend on its actual acceptance by the social group (but is something by which we may judge the actual morality of social groups), we have again to distinguish two different kinds of principle requiring the same action on a particular occasion. The area of morality I am attempting to delineate is that of principles which would lose their moral force unless they were widely accepted in a particular social group.

Promises constitute the obvious case of moral obligation, and here certainly we have all the three salient features that we have noticed. If we are to incur such obligations there must be some established procedure generally accepted by some specific social group whereby the utterance or writing of a certain range of expressions is sufficient to render actions specified by them obligatory for the speaker or writer. If no such procedures exist, promising is logically impossible, just as saluting would be logically impossible if there were no accepted conventions specifying the gestures of formal recognition within a military group. When we promise we make use of specified procedures in order to change the moral situation; in lawyer's language we exercise a "power" conferred by rules to change moral relations.

Promises have pre-eminently the feature I have called independence of content: the obligation springs not from the nature of the promised action but from the use of the procedure by the appropriate person in the appropriate circumstances. This independence is further manifested by the fact that the obligation thus deliberately created may also be deliberately extinguished by the promisee. This independence of content does not, however, entail that there is no restriction whatsoever upon the classes of action that a person may make obligatory for himself by promising to do them. Morals like law may have principles of "public policy" and render "void" a promise that from the start involved doing something patently immoral; but we should distinguish from such cases those where we subsequently discover moral reasons (perhaps in changed circumstances) against doing what we have promised to do. In these latter cases we have a moral obligation arising from the promise, but one that we consider in the light of other principles we ought not to carry out.

The third element of *coercion* needs careful scrutiny in this and other cases of moral obligation. In the case of legal obligation, rules typically provide that, in the event of failure or threatened failure to do what other primary rules require, there must be some official determination of the fact of this failure (judgment of a court) and then a variety of official steps taken to punish the failure or, in civil cases, to secure performance or its nearest equivalent. These steps include imprisonment used as punishment or used differently as a means of inducing obedience in a particular case or the forcible seizure of money or goods (execution) for compensation —and there are many other variants. By contrast (and this is one major distinction between moral and legal obligation), the coercion characteristic of moral obligation takes the form not of the infliction of harm or the use of force but primarily of the exposure of the individual to reminders that he has failed to comply with rules regarded by the social group as a matter of serious importance and to demand that he should comply. The typical moral pressure takes the form of an appeal not to fear of harmful consequences or to the futility of refusing to do what in the end one will be forced to do but to the delinquent's presumed respect for the rules he has broken. "You have broken your promise." "That would involve breaking your promise." The assumption inherent in such criticism is that what is most needed is a reminder of what the rules require and that the guilt or shame engendered by the contemplation of their breach will suffice or at least tend to inhibit future or continued failure to comply. Of course there are ancillary techniques: blame, praise, exhortation, severance of social relations, temporary exclusion from the group may be used, and these may shade off into something very like threats of harm and punishment. Yet, as soon as an appeal is made primarily to fear even of unorganized "sanctions," we are on the way from moral to legal obligation. The fact that moral pressure is characteristically exerted through an appeal to the delinquent's assumed respect for the institution violated, together with the fact that the plea, "I could not help it," is, if substantiated, always an excuse, jointly constitute the "internality" of morals as compared with the "externality" of law. This has sometimes been grossly misrepresented by the contention that whereas laws require us to do certain actions morals only require us to be in certain states of mind (or soul).

If we now consider not promises but the moral duties attached to an office or role in social life, these differ most notably in that the particular duties attached to these roles (a husband's duty to support his wife, the father's to look after his children) are not conceived of as truly created by the deliberate choice of the individual. The independence of content that these duties have is therefore rather different in that they are conceived of as *assumed* by entry upon the particular role so that one who takes up the role is thereby specially committed to discharging these duties. They are not principles of universal application to all societies alike but are conceived of as something that may vary from society to society together with a whole mass of associated institutions. Hence the obligation to maintain wife or children may not attach to husband or father in societies that think of it as normal for the wife to work and for children to be provided with support at the public expense. As noted above, though wider principles of morality may require a man to look after any child in need of care, the *duty* on a parent to do this springs from the fact that this particular society attaches moral importance to persons occupying such a position doing this.

If we consider the notion of a moral obligation to obey the law, we find that there are a number of issues requiring separation. One of them we have already discussed: viz., the claim that if a legal system exists then it follows that there must logically be a general recognition of moral obligation to obey the law so that if there is no such general recognition of a moral obligation to obey the law it would be a mistake to say that a legal system existed. Apart from this, however, there is some ambiguity in the notion of an obligation to obey *the law*. Presumably, if we consider that we should obey only those laws whose effects are likely to be (morally) good or the lesser of two (moral) evils, this would not be the recognition of a moral obligation to obey the law but only the application of some general principle that we should maximize good and minimize evil. The recognition of an obligation to obey *the law* must as a minimum imply that there is at least some area of conduct regulated by law in which we are not free to judge the moral merits of particular laws and to make our obedience conditional on this judgment. In a modern state it seems most plausible to suggest that this area is that which includes matters of defense and economic welfare but excludes, say, mat-

ters of religion or esthetic taste. Do we in fact recognize that
we are bound within some such area to obey the law as such?
There is at least a plausible argument that we do not in fact
recognize any such obligation to obey the law as such but that
our moral scruples against disobeying those laws whose effects
we may think bad is due to the consideration that our disobedience might encourage general disorder and would therefore be the greater of two evils. Yet, though plausible, this is
not convincing: it ignores, first, the fact that if we are ready
to go to prison rather than obey our attitudes might very well
strengthen the system as a whole and not weaken it; second,
it ignores the very important fact that obedience often appears to most not as something required by a general principle that we should not harm human beings unnecessarily
but as something required by the consideration that the particular members of our own society have obeyed the law and expect it to be obeyed. Where obedience to the law is motivated by such considerations, there is recognition of a moral
obligation to obey with the three salient features that characterize it.

IV

In conclusion, I shall shortly consider certain motives for
extending the use of "obligation" or "duty" to a much wider
field so as to include those principles by reference to which
we criticize adherence to or departures from the accepted
morality of a social group. In the little-read second and third
chapters of *The Province of Jurisprudence Determined*,
Austin described the area of morality with which I have been
concerned as that of "positive morality"; [11] with it he contrasted the Law of God, which constituted in his view the
proper standard for the criticism of both positive law and
positive morality and to which the principles of general utility

[11] Austin, *The Province of Jurisprudence Determined*, pp. 12 and
125–29.

are our "index." On such a view the ultimate principles of morality are the commands of God, and on this view we shall have no difficulty in conceiving of all the actions that they require as obligations. This is so because of the strength of the analogy between fundamental principles so conceived and the three salient features of obligation. For, first, fundamental moral principles on this view will be independent of content since they will owe their status not to what they require but to their being the commands of God. Second, God has every power and, on some accounts, every intention to punish disobedience or render it futile. But God's authority is not on such a view constituted by the actual practice of a social group, and it is this which renders the analogy imperfect so that the claim that "I have a moral obligation to do X" means the same as "God has commanded me to do X" may be a source of confusion even among those who share this view.

A very different motive for the extension of the concept of obligation is to be found in J. S. Mill's *Utilitarianism* [12] and probably still inspires most of those who wish to use the term widely. Mill says that

> . . . the idea of penal sanction, which is the essence of law, enters not only into the conception of injustice, but into that of any kind of wrong. We do not call anything wrong, unless we mean to imply that a person ought to be punished in some way or other for doing it; if not by law, by the opinion of his fellow-creatures; if not by opinion, by the reproaches of his own conscience. This seems the real turning point of the distinction between morality and simple expediency. It is a part of the notion of Duty in every one of its forms, that a person may rightfully be compelled to fulfil it.

Here, it seems to me, Mill very accurately fastens on the notion of coercion as essential to both legal and moral obligation, but this is accurate where coercion refers to the at-

[12] See J. S. Mill, *Utilitarianism* (Everyman's Library ed.; New York: E. P. Dutton & Co., 1910), chap. v, p. 45.

titudes or actions of other human beings and where compulsion has a similar meaning. There is, however, a step of some magnitude from the notion of being punished or compelled by "the law and the opinion of fellow creatures" to the notion of "punishment or compulsion by the reproaches of conscience." Some analogy there is; yet it may well be felt that its utility is limited, and that the line between all "morality" and "simple expediency" is far too complex to be drawn in this way.

G. E. HUGHES

Moral Condemnation

Sometimes we say of someone that he ought not to have done what he did; sometimes we say more generally that actions of a certain kind ought not to be done. When we say these things (and mean them), we are at least expressing our condemnation of the action in question, or of actions of the kind in question; and our condemnation in either case may be moral condemnation or nonmoral condemnation. But what is it to condemn something morally, as distinct from taking up some other unfavorable attitude toward it? And by what sort of rational argument, if any, can we try to persuade someone to condemn what he is at present inclined to condone, or to condone what he is at present inclined to condemn? These are the main questions I have had in mind while writing this paper.

I

First, what is moral condemnation? What is it, that is, to condemn something morally? It cannot be merely to say certain words, such as, "Smith ought not to have done that"; for I may say these words without meaning them, or even without understanding them. It might be suggested that it is to say such words *and mean them;* but this, even if true, is unenlightening, for *what it is to mean them* is precisely the problem we are concerned with.

Nor will it do to say that to condemn Smith's action morally is to have or express a certain emotion (say, of indignation) about what he did, or to say words such as, "Smith ought not to have done that" accompanied by or as an expression of such an emotion. For suppose that half an hour later the conversation turns to the case of Smith once more, and this time I say, "Smith was quite right to act as he did"; and suppose someone objects, "But half an hour ago you said he ought not to have done it"; and suppose I reply, "But half an hour ago I happened to feel indignant, so naturally I said he ought not to have done what he did; now, however, I don't happen to feel indignant any longer, so equally naturally I say he was quite right to do it"—suppose I behave like that, then if the analysis we are considering is correct I shall be said to have been condemning Smith's action morally at time t_1 and exonerating it at time t_2, half an hour later. And, again if the analysis is correct, there will be nothing odd about this, for people commonly do calm down in even less than half an hour. The correct comment, however, if I behave in the way I have described, ought to be that I was not making a *moral* judgment at either time t_1 or time t_2. Certainly a man may *change his mind,* about a moral matter as well as about any other, but it will be comparatively easy to see whether I have changed my mind between time t_1 and time t_2. For one condition which must be fulfilled if I am to be said to have changed my mind is that at time t_2 I must be willing to retract the condemnation of Smith's action which I made at time t_1, and that not merely in the sense that I no longer condemn it now but in the stronger sense that I now admit that I was mistaken in condemning it then. And I shall have to be willing to support my retraction of my condemnation by mentioning features of Smith's action or of its attendant circumstances of which I was previously ignorant, or to which I now attach more weight than I did then, or by referring to moral principles under which I now see Smith's action to be subsumable, and so forth; but *not* by merely pointing out that I have now cooled down. In the conversation reported above, it is I hope clear that I had not changed my mind at time t_2 (if this is not clear I have reported the conversation badly); my mood had changed, but that is quite a different matter.

It would make no difference to the argument of the last paragraph if someone were to say that the emotion in question—the indignation or whatever it was—was of a special "moral" kind, if by that is meant that it had a certain introspectively distinguishable "tone" which we can label "moral." I mean that it still will not do to say that to condemn something morally is to have or express an emotion of this introspectively distinguishable sort, even if there is such a sort. My argument would I think hold good whatever the nuances of my emotional states might have been in the case described. I know it is sometimes debated whether there is an introspectively distinguishable moral emotional tone; but the question, "Does moral indignation *feel different* from nonmoral indignation?" is an empirical question of interest to the psychologist rather than to the moral philosopher, and in any case it presupposes that we can distinguish moral from nonmoral indignation otherwise than by what they feel like. I think we usually use the phrase "moral indignation" to mean "indignation (whatever precisely it feels like) that is directed toward what we morally condemn"; and if it is not always used in that way I think it would conduce to clarity so to use it. If it is used in this way, then the question, "Is my indignation moral indignation?" could not be answered by introspection of the feeling. Moreover, the occurrence of the dialogue reported above would be evidence that my indignation at time t_1 was *not* moral indignation (and that whatever it felt like introspectively); and in that case it would be senseless to try to counter the argument by saying, "But suppose the indignation were of a special moral kind. . . ."

(We could go through an analogous refutation of the thesis that to make a moral judgment is simply to issue a command.)

We must be careful here, however. It is tempting, and not merely tempting but helpful, to reformulate the question, "What is moral condemnation?" as, "What am I doing when I condemn something morally?" But if this is taken to mean "What am I *doing* when I condemn something morally? what is going on in me at such a time?" then the reformulation can be dangerous. For, if we try to observe carefully what we are doing or what is going on in us when we are inclined to describe ourselves as condemning something morally, then indeed it may very well be that all that we can detect is that we say the words and have the feeling (and it may even be less than that). And, if we have been convinced by the previous argument that to condemn something morally is not, or is not merely, to say the words and have the feeling, then we may be tempted to come to the conclusion that we were not engaging in moral condemnation when we thought we were. And this would be an unwarranted conclusion (even though it *is* possible to think one is condemning something morally when one is not). What we ought rather to say, I think, is that even when nothing relevant is "going on" except saying the words and having the feeling, yet I still in spite of that may be condemning Smith's action morally; and that whether I am doing so or not will depend (to speak very schematically for the moment) on what I regard myself as committed to by saying the words I do.

II

The phrase "committed to," which I have just used, stands in need of elucidation, however; and most of the rest of this paper will be concerned in one way or another with the attempt to elucidate it. The problem in this connection to which I want to direct attention at present may be put in the following way: Jones has just said, "Smith ought not to have done what he did," or "it would be wrong to do X" (where X stands for a certain *kind* of action); what discoveries about Jones—his words, actions, thoughts, dispositions—would lead someone to say, "So Jones wasn't really morally condemning Smith's action (or X) after all; he was just annoyed, or using words wildly, or being insincere"?

Let us consider an example in which what is condemned is a certain kind of action (we shall return to the condemnation of particular actions later). Suppose during a conversation one Wednesday evening Jones says in our presence, "It's wrong to join the army." On Thursday morning, however, we are passing the recruiting office and we see Jones on the point of enlisting. We had not expected this. True, Jones hadn't *said* he would not enlist, but still, what he did say led us to expect that he would not. Did he really mean what he said last night, we wonder. So we say to him, "I thought you said last night that it was wrong to join the army." Among the responses that Jones may make to this are the following:

1. He may say, "Yes, but I've been doing some hard thinking overnight, and I have come to the conclusion that I was mistaken"—and then go on to mention facts about military service or the international situation. This is a straightforward case of a change of mind or opinion on a moral matter. (With the question of how or whether the change of mind is to be justified we are not at present concerned.)

2. Jones may reply, "Yes, but my case is a special one." Such a reply may strike us as suspicious, but it may yet be redeemed. "In what way?" we ask; and he goes on to point out certain features of his own case that do not apply to most other people. "I meant last night," he concludes, "that *in general* it is wrong to join the army; of course there are exceptions, and

my case is one. I could have gone into this last night, but
someone changed the subject." Now his reasons for regarding
his own case as a special one may or may not be good ones
(that is not what we are discussing at the moment), but there
is nothing in principle absurd about the line his argument
takes here. There are, however, two important points to be
noted: (a) What Jones is doing is not keeping to his original
principle but admitting exceptions to it, but rather modifying
his principle or at least saying that his original formulation of
it was defective. He is now saying that the principle to which
he really adheres is one of the form, "It is wrong to do X except in certain specific types of circumstance," and he is
claiming that his own action in enlisting does not violate this
rule because his own circumstances are among those covered
in the exceptive clause. (There is, of course, nothing wrong
with such a form for a moral rule; indeed, probably most of
the prohibitory moral rules to which we adhere are of this
form.) Jones may not be able to find a precise formulation of
the specifiable circumstances in question that will satisfy him,
and that may be why he uses the vague formula, "*in general*
it's wrong to. . . ." We commonly do say, "In general it is
wrong to do X, but there are exceptions," meaning thereby
to express our adherence to a more complicated rule which (as
is often the case) we are uncertain how to formulate. But it
should be noted that we do not mean that this more complicated rule is one that has exceptions: what falls under an
exceptive clause *within* a rule does not constitute an exception
to the rule. (b) If Jones is to maintain his claim to be morally
condemning X, even "in general" (in the sense explained), he
must be willing to display some practical antiattitudes toward
some actions of kind X. He must be willing, for example, to
discourage at least certain classes of people from doing X, or
to contribute to the relief of those who suffer because of their
refusal to do X, or something of that kind; and his motives in
doing these things would be relevant too. Just how many dis-

plays of such antiattitudes he must give in order to justify his claim to be morally condemning X is a nice point that I shall not attempt to discuss here; but at least if he gives none at all there is no substance left in his claim. For in what would his being *against* X then consist, and how can one condemn anything morally without being against it?

3. Jones may look shamefaced and say, "I'm afraid I haven't got much moral fiber; I can't bring myself to do unpopular things." In this case, whatever our judgment on Jones's will-power may be, logically at least we are happy again. He has not changed his mind this time, as in case 1 (which would be one way of making us logically happy); nor has he modified his formulation of his rule as in case 2 (which would be another way); but he has in a third way removed our doubts as to whether he "meant what he said" on the previous evening, our doubts as to whether he was then really morally condemning joining the army. For he is ready to condemn his own action as he does it. After all, he not merely did not say on Wednesday that he would not join the army, he did not say anything that entailed that he would not. Even if he had said explicitly, "I believe it's wrong to join the army, but I am going to enlist tomorrow," he would not have been contradicting himself. Only we should note that he would not have been likely to use the noncommittal conjunction "and" but rather the adversative "but." For although "I believe it's wrong to join the army" does not entail the falsity of "I'm going to enlist tomorrow," the two statements are not completely logically independent of each other either. The truth of the second does tell against (though not *conclusively* against) the first's being an expression of moral condemnation. Any utterance of the form, "I believe it is wrong to do X, but I am going to do it" is what we might call a "logical eyebrow-raiser": we want the man who says it to tell us more before we can be quite sure that he understands what he is saying. But he may be able to do the filling in to our satisfaction; and the filling in may

consist in explaining that, although he is not to be expected to display that particular antiattitude toward X which consists in avoiding X, yet he may be expected to display that other antiattitude toward X which consists in feeling ashamed of himself if and when he does X.

There is a further point to be noted here. I have been speaking as if feeling ashamed of oneself for doing an action of kind X constituted a condemning of that action, and so in a way it does: it is *some* kind of condemnation, and it is certainly one of the things we take into account in support of the claim that the agent morally condemns actions of kind X. But it would be a mistake simply to identify the feeling of shame with *moral* condemnation either of that particular action or of actions of that general kind. This point can be brought out by comparing two questions: (a) Does "Jones morally condemns actions of kind X and knows he is now doing an action of kind X" entail "Jones morally condemns his present action"? and (b) Does the same premise entail "Jones has feelings of shame or guilt in respect of his present action"? I think it is clear that the answer to (a) is, Yes, but that the answer to (b) is, No; it would be possible for Jones to condemn his present action morally yet have no *feelings* of shame. No doubt feelings of shame are very commonly present when we morally condemn our own actions, but this is not necessarily so. So, although Jones's feelings of shame as he does X and knows he does X are evidence, and even good evidence, that he morally condemns actions of kind X, they are dispensable. What is not dispensable is that he should morally condemn his present action. But, of course, *what it is to condemn his present action morally* is at the present stage of our discussion problematic in a way in which *what it is to feel ashamed of himself* is not. To say that one thing that is required if a man is to be said morally to condemn actions of kind X is that if he does such an action and knows he does it he must morally condemn that action, while true, is quite unenlightening. We could, however, add this: that a man who said, "It's wrong to do X," did an action of kind X, and did not feel ashamed of himself might begin to restore our shaken confidence in his moral condemnation of X by displaying signs of a resolution to avoid doing X in the future. Indeed we might well take this as *more than making up for* his lack of feelings of shame.

4. But suppose—to skip a number of other possibilities and jump to the most extreme one—we find that Jones not merely fails to display shame at his own action in enlisting, but would not feel indignant at anyone for enlisting, would not discourage anyone from joining the army, would not resolve not to join the army a second time, would not in fact display *any* antiattitude toward any act of enlistment. What are we to make of this? Surely he *must* have changed his mind. We ask him; but he says he has not, and for good measure he is willing to go on repeating the words, "It's wrong to join the army," as often as we wish. But now this *is* logically absurd. Indeed the point of absurdity comes long before this extreme case, but it comes out most glaringly here. He may be using the words, "It's wrong . . . ," in some private sense of his own that we have not divined; they may (for all we can tell) be some phrase in Swahili that he keeps on repeating because he likes the sound of it; but he is not using them to express any condemnation of anything, let alone any *moral* condemnation. And, if he claims that we were not justified in concluding from what he said on the previous evening that he would *either* refrain from enlisting *or* display shame if he did enlist *or* . . . , then he was not using the phrase, "It's wrong . . . ," to express a condemnation on that occasion either.

We might sum up what emerges from our discussion of this example as follows: If I am to maintain my claim to be using a sentence of the form "It's wrong to do X" to express a moral condemnation, I must either be willing to refrain from doing X or feel ashamed of myself if I do X or resolve not to do X again if I do it once or discourage some others

from doing X or feel ashamed of myself if I do not so discourage them or. . . . (I make no attempt to complete the
list of relevant antiattitudes, but I think I have mentioned
the most important ones.) No one of these is necessary to the
maintaining of my claim, but total failure (and indeed something less than total failure) to display any of them is fatal
to my claim. We could speak of what is required to maintain
my claim as the displaying of an "adequate set of the relevant
antiattitudes," but it would not, I think, be possible to specify
exactly what would constitute such an adequate set of them,
though we could easily think of sets that were and sets that
were not adequate.

To this must be added the following remark: It is not any
and every refraining from doing X that would count as evidence that I was using "It is wrong to do X" to express moral
condemnation. The question of *why* I refrain is crucial. If
I were to refrain simply because I foresaw that the results of
doing X would be unpleasant for myself, that would not count;
if I were to refrain simply in order to try to convince the person to whom I said, "It's wrong to do X" that I *was* condemning X morally, that would not count either. The question,
What motives for refraining *would* count? would take us too
far afield at present, but some hints of an answer to it will, I
hope, be extractable from subsequent pages.

III

Let us now turn to the kind of case in which what is condemned is a particular action that has been done. I think of
what Smith did; I say, "Smith ought not to have done that"
(or, "It was wrong of Smith to do that"); and perhaps I feel
a wave of indignation as or just before I say it. The question
is, how can we distinguish between my saying what I say
merely as an expression of the emotion I feel at the time (and
perhaps will not feel half an hour hence) and my saying the

same words as a moral condemnation of what Smith did. We saw near the beginning of this paper that one condition that has to be fulfilled if I am to be said to be using the words as a moral condemnation is that I must be willing to go on saying them even after I have cooled down, unless in the interval I have had some new relevant information or thoughts about what Smith did. But this is certainly not sufficient; and our more recent discussion would seem to indicate that one further condition (I do not say the only further condition) that has to be fulfilled is my either refusing to do myself what Smith did, or being ready to blame myself if I do so, or discouraging others from doing what Smith did, or . . . ; some adequate set of these. Only there is a difficulty here, for neither I nor anyone else will ever be in a position to do exactly what Smith did. So instead of "what Smith did" we shall have to say something like "any action that resembles what Smith did in the relevant respects"—or rather, I think, "any action that I consider to resemble what Smith did in the relevant respects." (The point of my preference for the latter of these two phrases will become clearer later on.) The crucial word here is the word "relevant," and in the attempt to elucidate what it means in this context we shall I hope gain a clearer understanding of what it is to condemn something morally, as well as some insight into an important type of moral argument. The immediate point I am making, however, is simply that the man who condemns some particular action but who does not regard this condemnation as committing him to condemning any other action, actual or possible, is thereby showing that his condemnation is not *moral* condemnation. (To point this out is to give part of the analysis of what is meant by the word "moral.") It is not so with all kinds of antiattitudes. It is not so with dislike, for example. I may just happen to dislike what Smith did and not dislike anything resembling it; your discovery that this is so may lead you to regard me as an unpredictable person and difficult to get on with, but it certainly does not entitle you to draw the conclusion that I did not or do not really dislike what Smith did. It may leave you puzzled about *why* I dislike it, but that is another matter.

The questions that seem to call for discussion here are these: What is it to regard one action as like another in the "morally relevant respects"? To what other actions does a man by morally condemning one particular action commit himself also to condemn (this is the same question in another form)? And, In what sense is the word "commit" being used here? We mentioned the last of these questions earlier, but we have certainly not given a satisfactory answer to it yet. I propose to tackle these questions by considering a certain kind of moral argument.

We sometimes say to a man: "Since you condemn what A did you must in consistency also condemn what B did or is proposing to do"; and sometimes we say this even when A's and B's actions are on the face of it pretty dissimilar, though doubtless not when they are *very* dissimilar. A remark like this should perhaps not be called an *argument*; it is more like the hint of an argument that we hope we shall not have to go to the trouble of producing in full. It is the nature of the kind of argument of which such a remark is a hint that I want to look into.

Let us suppose, then, that Macdonald and I are discussing something that Macdonald is proposing to do. Let us suppose that Macdonald and I are in complete agreement about the empirical characteristics of what he proposes to do and the circumstances in which he proposes to do it; but I am prepared to condemn what he proposes to do, whereas he thinks he is entitled to do it. Let us suppose, too, that there is another action, done by O'Reilly, about the empirical characteristics of which Macdonald and I are again in agreement; and let us suppose that Macdonald and I both condemn what O'Reilly did. Let us suppose, finally, that if I were to draw up a list of the similarities and another list of the differences between what O'Reilly did and what Macdonald proposes to do, Macdonald would assent to every item on my two lists and would have nothing to add to either of them. My aim is to use Macdonald's admission that he condemns what O'Reilly did to induce him to condemn what he himself proposes to do. (In what follows I shall use the small letters "o" and "m" as abbreviations for "O'Reilly's action" and "Macdonald's action," respectively; and I shall use the capital letters "O" and "M" for "O'Reilly's action and its attendant circumstances" and "Macdonald's action and its attendant circumstances," respectively.)

I begin my argument by asking Macdonald to consider O and to tell me what are the characteristics of O that he takes into account in condemning o. By "those characteristics that he takes into account in condemning o" I do not mean those characteristics that he actually noticed when he uttered his condemnation of o; I mean rather those characteristics of O the removal or modification of which would lead him (Macdonald) to modify his condemnation of o or even withdraw it altogether, as distinct from those whose presence or absence would not influence his condemnation at all. Let us call such a characteristic "a Macdonald-ground of condemnation of o." Suppose now that, when we have discovered what the Macdonald-grounds of condemnation of o are (let us say there are two of them, a and b), we find that they are all (both) in our agreed list of similarities between O and M. (This is not as wild an assumption as it sounds: in the argument I am imagining it is I who bring up O as an example, and I choose it hoping that things will turn out thus. If they do not, I am at liberty to begin again with a new example.)

My next move is to point out that this is so. I say, "You condemn o in virtue of the fact that O possesses a and b. But M also possesses a and b. So you ought in consistency to condemn m also."

It is clear, I think, that Macdonald must either capitulate

immediately and agree to condemn *m*, or else to avoid doing so he must point to some characteristic—*c*—of M that it does not share with O and claim to regard that as a ground of exoneration, i.e., as a factor to be taken into consideration when deciding whether to condemn or exonerate, and one that tells in the direction of exoneration. (A third move that Macdonald might make instead is to resurvey O and discover in it a Macdonald-ground of condemnation that he had missed in his previous survey and that it does not share with M; but I shall neglect this possibility, as it raises no new issues of principle and would only complicate our account.) We can express the principle underlying this stage of the argument by saying that, when I morally condemn a given action and single out a set of characteristics of it and/or its attendant circumstances as my grounds of condemnation of it, I am thereby committing myself to condemning, not indeed any and every action which (or whose attendant circumstances) has these characteristics, but any and every such action *unless* it has some other characteristic that I am prepared to regard as relevant—and this time relevant as a ground of exoneration. (We shall look into what is involved in regarding something as a ground of exoneration in a moment.) This is because what Macdonald or I or anyone else picks out as a ground of condemnation is always a *characteristic*, and a characteristic is something that may have other instances beside the one I am considering. It would, I think, make no sense to advance "this particular instance of such and such a characteristic, but heaven knows what about any other instance of it" as a ground of condemnation.

Suppose, then, that Macdonald points to some characteristic *c* of M and says, "I regard that as a relevant difference between O and M, so my condemnation of *o* does not commit me to a condemnation of *m*." The question we have to elucidate here is, "What is Macdonald claiming when he claims to regard *c* as a relevant characteristic of M—relevant this time in the direction of exonerating *m*?" As far as I can see, he is claiming two things: (1) that if *c* were to be absent from M his attitude of condemnation-or-exoneration of *m* would change; and (2) that in other cases than M which also possess *c* he will take *c* into account in deciding whether to condemn or exonerate: i.e., if he exonerates *m* on account of *c* he will be prepared to exonerate in other cases where *c* is present *unless* some further characteristic is also present which again he regards as relevant; and so forth.

Now it is clear that a man may claim to regard a certain characteristic as relevant and be wrong in what he claims; i.e., he may claim that he regards it as relevant and yet not in fact regard it as relevant. (I am not now thinking of a distinction between something's being *really* relevant and its being merely *regarded as* relevant, but of the different distinction between someone's *actually* regarding it as relevant and that person's merely *claiming* to regard it as relevant.) And this may happen either through deceit or through honest mistake. That it may happen through deceit is obvious enough. But it is equally clear on reflection that it may happen through honest mistake; for Macdonald may think that the absence of *c* would change his attitude to *m* and yet find on further reflection that it would do no such thing; and he may think that he would be prepared to exonerate in other cases in which *c* is found and yet discover that when such cases are presented to him he is prepared to do no such thing. And this is where—to return to my argument with Macdonald—my next move comes in.

This next move might take either of two forms: (1) I might invite Macdonald to consider a case like M except that it does not have *c*, or at least like M in all other respects than *c* which Macdonald claims to regard as relevant, and to report whether his attitude of condemnation-or-exoneration differs or does not differ from his attitude to *m*. This is the less exciting direction my move may take; probably Macdonald will seldom be caught

in this simple way, though perhaps occasionally he may be.
(2) I might present for Macdonald's consideration a completely new case, which does however, like M, possess c, but
which I think Macdonald is likely to condemn. Macdonald
may indeed surprise me by exonerating in this new case too,
and then I shall have to try again with a new example. Or
Macdonald may, as I expect, condemn in the new case. If
he does, then if he is unable to point to some further characteristic d of the new case and claim to regard that as relevant,
I can retort: "So it turns out that you do not in fact regard c
as relevant to the exoneration or condoning of actions; so you
must condemn m after all"; but if he is able to point to some
characteristic d of the new case and claim to regard it as
relevant, then I can repeat my move: i.e., present him with a
still further case, possessing d this time, and see whether he
is prepared to go through with regarding d consistently as a
ground of condemnation of actions that possess it.

It is impossible to set a theoretical limit to the number of
stages in an argument of this kind. There may in fact in a
given case be no end, and the whole matter may be left inconclusive. This may be due to the fact that I (Macdonald's ad-
versary) am unskillful in my choice of examples or lacking in
dialectical acumen; but it may not: it may be due to the fact
that Macdonald's condemnings and condonings, while consistent among themselves, are very different from mine. In
fact, if they are very different indeed I may not be able to
start, i.e., to find a suitable O. But my aim is to bring the
argument to a termination, and to bring it to a termination
by making Macdonald see that in order to condemn o and condone m he would have to be prepared to condemn something
that he is not in fact prepared to condemn or to condone something that he is not in fact prepared to condone. It is true
that in a sense I have given Macdonald an infinite number of
theoretical escapes, and thus allowed him theoretically always
to protract the argument indefinitely; for I have allowed him

to name any characteristic of M he chooses (other than a and b) as one in virtue of which he regards m as permissible or exonerable, and it is *logically* possible for Macdonald to go on consistently regarding *any* such characteristic as a relevant one. But it may not always be practically possible for him to do so, or he may be practically unwilling to do so. For—and this is crucial to our understanding of the argument as a *moral* argument, i.e., as one species of practical argument as distinct from a purely theoretical argument—each of these escapes, each of these claimings to regard a characteristic as relevant, involves the adoption of some practical attitude toward an action or set of actions; and among the infinitely wide range of attitudes that it is logically conceivable that Macdonald should adopt, there will be many that he will be unwilling or unable to adopt. And, if I can show that the price of regarding m as morally legitimate is to regard c as a relevant ground of exoneration, and that the price of so regarding c is the adoption of some attitude that he, Macdonald, is unwilling or unable to adopt, then I have thereby shown that in consistency Macdonald must agree to condemn m.

The above account may appear complex; but it would be truer to say that it is oversimplified and overschematic. Macdonald's possible moves and countermoves are in fact more varied than I have indicated. I can only plead that I have been concerned with the general nature of such arguments rather than with their intricacies. What I am doing when I conduct such an argument might be generally described as facing Macdonald with the demand that he should bring a certain kind of *consistency* into his system of condemnings and condonings. And this demand seems to me to be justified on the ground that if Macdonald rejects it this is tantamount to an admission that his condemnings and condonings are not *moral* ones at all. I have been assuming throughout that Macdonald does not wish to admit this; but if he does, if he tries to evade my whole argument by saying, "I never make moral judgments anyway," I shall have to preface my argument with an argument of a different nature, designed to show that he does sometimes make moral judgments. I shall not discuss the nature of such an argument here, but there is no reason to think it might not sometimes be successful.

IV

There is an instructive example of a moral argument of the kind I have been discussing to be found in the Old Testament, in the story of David and Bathsheba. For the full account the reader is referred to chapters 11 and 12 of the Second Book of Samuel. Here the following summary must suffice.

David, King of Israel, in order to obtain the beautiful Bathsheba as his wife, arranged for the death of her husband Uriah in the following way: Uriah was on service with the army at the time, and David sent a message to the commanding officer instructing him to place Uriah where the fighting was thickest and then order his troops to retire from around him. All went according to David's plan: Uriah fell in battle, and Bathsheba became David's wife. But when the prophet Nathan heard what had happened he visited David and recounted to him an incident in which a wealthy landowner with large flocks of sheep, finding himself with an unexpected guest, prepared a meal for him by killing not one of his own sheep but the one and only pet lamb belonging to a poor neighbor. David was moved to indignation by this narrative and demanded the name of the offender; whereupon Nathan replied, "It is you," and proceeded to draw the parallels between the story he had just told and David's treatment of Uriah.

It is recorded that David saw the point of Nathan's argument and came to condemn his own behavior toward Uriah. But to see the nature of the argument more clearly it will be convenient to neglect this recorded outcome and ask, "How could David, had he wished to do so, maintain his condemnation of the man in Nathan's parable and yet condone his own conduct toward Uriah?" What replies could David have made to Nathan had he wished to do this? (It will be convenient to have names for the characters in Nathan's story; let us call the rich man Simeon and the poor man Issachar.)

1. David may say, "I feel indignant when I think about Simeon's treatment of Issachar; I just do not feel indignant when I think about my own treatment of Uriah." David may say this, and indeed it may be true. But the price he has to pay for saying this is to admit that his "condemnation" of Simeon is now merely an introspective report of his feelings and not a moral condemnation at all. This, however, we can suppose he wishes to avoid admitting. To avoid admitting it he must point to some difference between the two cases and claim to regard it as relevant. There is no lack of differences and similarities between the two cases: part of Nathan's technique consisted in selecting a story sufficiently like David's behavior to enable him to draw the parallel but sufficiently unlike it to prevent David from seeing his game too soon.

2. Suppose David chooses one of the differences and says, "But I am a king, and Simeon is not." The force of such a remark would seem to be as follows: David admits that he would condemn his treatment of Uriah if it were done by someone other than the king, but regards the fact that the agent is a king as a ground of exoneration. Kings may do what they like, at least in the matter of acquiring wives, to put it roughly. But is David seriously willing to go through with the business of regarding kingship as an exonerating characteristic? Nathan might try as a reply: "So I take it that if and when the king of —— conquers the land of Israel and proposes to treat you much as you treated Uriah, you having done nothing more to harm him than Uriah did to harm you, you will have no condemnation for his action?"—and this may give David food for thought. Or, if Nathan is in a more analytic mood, he may

try: "Yes, but please be more explicit. What constitutes being a king? What characteristic of kinghood have you in mind as an exonerating factor? Is it power, or the habitual obedience rendered by the bulk of a given society (if we allow Nathan to anticipate Austin [1]), or what?" And, taking David's own choice of characteristic, he may proceed much as before.

It would be tedious to go through other differences that David might adduce between the two cases. But it is perhaps worth noting that there is one answer that David cannot make, and that is, "But I am I and he is someone else." No doubt many of us are tempted to make such a rejoinder in cases of this kind, but the remark is of course perfectly vacuous. It is not to mention a characteristic at all, far less to claim to regard a characteristic as relevant. Even the remark, "But I am David and he is Simeon," *names* the parties without informing us of their characteristics (except the trivial one that they are called by those names—trivial because the task of showing that David does not regard his own name as an exonerating characteristic is too easy to be worth tackling seriously). This, I think, is one way of showing what is wrong with "making an exception in one's own favor" in morals. I mean, of course, "making an exception in one's own favor just because one is oneself"; to make an exception in one's own case because one has certain characteristics is quite a different matter: that is something quite impersonal, for these characteristics may be possessed by others, and one may come to lose them oneself.

V

I undertook the discussion of relevant characteristics and arguing from condemnation of one action to condemnation of another in order to cast some light on the concept of moral

[1] J. Austin, *Lectures on Jurisprudence*, rev. and ed. by Robert Campbell (2 vols.; 4th ed.; London: John Murray, 1873), I, 226.

condemnation itself. I began by saying that if a man condemns some particular action done by, say, Smith, but does not regard this condemning as committing him to condemning any other action, actual or conceivable, then his condemnation of what Smith did will not count as *moral* condemnation. (It would more accurately be described as his being annoyed with Smith or feeling uncomfortable at the thought of what Smith did or something of that kind.) I next said that by morally condemning a particular action one is committed to condemning any other action that one regards as similar to that action in the relevant respects. I now want to try to make all this more precise.

We can offer an account of what it is to say that A regards Y as similar to X in the relevant respects in the following way. ("X" and "Y" are to be understood here as denoting particular actions, not kinds of actions; and for the sake of simplicity I shall assume throughout that X is an action that A condemns, though not necessarily *morally* condemns.)

Using a term I introduced earlier, I shall first define "an A-ground of condemnation of X" as any characteristic that A believes X (or its attendant circumstances) to possess and that he takes into account as something in virtue of which he condemns X. Now any A-ground of condemnation of X, or any set of such grounds, may be either *sufficient* or *insufficient*. I shall say that it is *sufficient* if A would still condemn X even if he believed it did not possess any of the other A-grounds of condemnation of X; and I shall say that such a ground or set of grounds is *insufficient* if A would withdraw his condemnation if he believed that X possessed only that ground or set of grounds and not any of the others. Among the A-grounds of condemnation of X there may (or may not) be several sufficient grounds or sets of grounds, and the sufficient sets of grounds, if there are any, may (or may not) overlap.

We can now say that A regards Y as similar to X in the relevant respects if and only if he believes (1) that some sufficient A-ground (or set of A-grounds) of condemnation of X is also possessed by Y, and also believes (2) that Y does *not* possess any further characteristic that he is prepared to cite as an A-ground of exoneration of Y and that he believes he would be prepared to count as a ground of exoneration (not necessarily a sufficient one) of any other action that possessed it.

It is important to see what this account does and does not state. It amounts to this: In order to claim that he does *not* regard Y as similar to X in the relevant respects, A must *either* maintain that Y does not possess any of the sufficient A-grounds (or sets of A-grounds) of condemnation of X, *or* cite some characteristic of Y (or its attendant circumstances) that is not possessed by X. But it will not be sufficient for him to cite *any* characteristic of Y not possessed by X; for there will always be such characteristics, and if he were allowed to cite any of these without restriction he could claim that he *never* regarded two actions as similar in the relevant respects. So I have added the restriction that the characteristic he cites must be one that he believes he would be willing to regard as a ground of exoneration wherever it is found. Note that I do *not* say, "that he *would* be willing to regard as a ground of exoneration wherever it is found"; but only "that he *believes* he would be willing to regard. . . ." So long as A believes he would be willing to regard the characteristic he cites as such a ground of exoneration, I shall say that he regards Y as *not* similar to X in the relevant respects. He may of course discover on reflection or experiment that his belief was incorrect, that he would not in fact be prepared to regard the characteristic in question as a ground of exoneration wherever it is found. But then he no longer has that belief, and so (unless he cites yet *another* characteristic of Y) I shall say that he has now ceased to regard Y as not similar to X in the relevant respects.

It is important, too, to notice that my account of what it

is for A to regard Y as similar to X in the relevant respects has
not contained any reference to whether A condemns Y. It is
perfectly possible for a man to condemn X, to regard Y as
similar to X in the relevant respects, and yet not to condemn
Y; in fact this not infrequently happens, especially when X
is someone else's action and Y one of our own or one done by
someone in whom we are specially interested. *But now my
contention is that it is logically absurd to say,* "A *morally* condemns X, regards Y as similar to X in the relevant respects,
but does not condemn Y." In other words, the relation I expressed earlier by the words "being committed to" is a relation
of logical commitment, not one of moral commitment. It is
not that the man who morally condemns some action but
fails to condemn what he regards as like it in the relevant respects is behaving immorally, but rather that the statement,
"A morally condemns X but does not condemn what he regards as relevantly like X," is logically absurd—for his condemnation of X in these circumstances would not be *moral*
condemnation. (There are moral commitments as well as logical ones in this context, but I shall defer mention of them
till later.)

I am maintaining, then, that whereas the sentence, (1)
"Whoever condemns X also condemns whatever he regards
as similar to X in the relevant respects," expresses a contingent
(and incidentally false) proposition, the sentence, (2) "Whoever *morally* condemns X also morally condemns whatever
he regards as similar to X in the relevant respects," expresses
a logically necessary truth, and one that is elucidatory, or at
least partially elucidatory, of the meaning of the word
"morally."

There is however a third sentence, which might be confused
with (2) but which does not express a logically necessary
truth any more than (1) does. To explain what this is I shall
introduce a new expression to contrast with "A regards Y as
similar to X in the relevant respects." I shall say that Y *is in*

fact relevantly similar to X *relative to* A's *system of valuation* if and only if the following conditions are fulfilled: (a) Y (or its attendant circumstances) *in fact* possesses some sufficient A-ground (or set of A-grounds) of condemnation of X; and (b) Y *in fact* fails to possess any characteristic that A *would* be prepared to regard as a ground of exoneration wherever it was found. (Again I have for simplicity confined myself to the case in which A *condemns* X.) And now the sentence to which I have referred, which does *not* express a necessary truth is, (3) "Whoever morally condemns X also morally condemns whatever is in fact relevantly similar to X relative to his system of valuation." (If we were to use the word "morally" in such a way that [3] did express a necessary truth, we should have to say that only a man who is in possession of all relevant information and who is completely clear-headed can [logically] ever make judgments of moral condemnation at all; and this would be a preposterous way to use the word "morally" and the phrase "moral condemnation.") It is clear that Y may be in fact relevantly similar to X relative to A's system of valuation without A's realizing that it is. In such a case, although there is a sense in which we can say that A is "committed in all consistency" to condemning Y morally if he condemns X morally, yet we cannot say he is committed to doing so in the sense that if he does not do so his condemnation of X will not count as *moral* condemnation. A has to be brought to *believe* that Y is relevantly similar to X relative to his system of valuation if he is to be committed in *that* way: that, indeed, is the point of the kind of moral argument I was discussing earlier in this paper.

There is a partial analogy that may help to make this clearer. Suppose that we have two propositions, *p* and *q*, and that *p* entails *q*. We should be inclined to say that anyone who believes *p* is logically committed to believing *q*, too. But we should be careful about what is meant by this: for clearly the man who claims to believe *p* and to disbelieve *q*, *failing* to see that p entails q, does not commit the same absurdity as the man who claims to believe p and to disbelieve q while admitting that p entails q. The logical absurdity involved in saying, "A believes p, sees that p entails q, and disbelieves q" is such that we should be entitled to say that A's disbelief of q plus his recognition that p entails q is adequate ground for denying that he really believes p (or, alternatively, that his belief in p plus his recognition that p entails q is adequate ground for denying that he really disbelieves q). But the muddle-headed B who fails to see that p entails q at all does not commit *this* absurdity in claiming to believe p and disbelieve q. In *his* case, while we might advance the fact that he disbelieves q plus the fact that p entails q as ground for saying that he ought not to believe p, we could not advance it as ground for saying that he *does not* believe p. In a somewhat similar way, we can advance the fact that a man does not condemn actions that he regards as relevantly similar to X as a ground for saying that his condemnation of X is not moral condemnation; but we cannot advance the fact that he fails to condemn actions that in fact are relevantly similar to X relative to his system of valuation, though he does not realize that they are, as a ground for saying that his condemnation of X is not moral condemnation.

Someone may say to me: "You have spoken so far merely of actions as being relevantly alike relative to someone's system of valuation. But can we speak of actions as being *really* alike in the relevant respects, or alike in the *really* relevant respects, without reference to any particular person's system of valuation?" I think something can be done to form such a concept, though whether it would satisfy my imaginary questioner is another matter. Again, for simplicity, I shall assume that X is condemned. We might say that Y *is really similar to* X *in the relevant respects* if the following conditions are fulfilled:

1. There is some characteristic or set of characteristics of X or its attendant circumstances that (a) anyone capable of coherent thinking about morals would regard as a ground of

condemnation of X, and (b) is in fact also possessed by Y or its attendant circumstances.

2. Y or its attendant circumstances in fact possesses no other characteristic that anyone capable of coherent thinking about morals would in fact be prepared consistently to regard as a ground of exoneration wherever it is found.

Whether there is any pair of actions that satisfy these conditions I do not know; and this is partly because the definition I have given contains a highly problematic phrase, viz., "anyone capable of coherent thinking about morals." How should we decide whether a given person was or was not capable of coherent thinking about morals? Partly, no doubt, we should use empirical tests, but our decision would also rest partly on a moral judgment on our own part; and even the empirical criteria are by no means as clear-cut as one might wish. My definition might certainly be criticized on this score, and I must admit that I do not know how to amend it to meet such an objection. But, if this criticism is waived, then, if there are two actions X and Y that fulfill the conditions set down, we can say that anyone who morally condemns X ought in consistency to condemn Y, too, in a sense analogous to that in which anyone who believes *p* ought in consistency to believe whatever is entailed by *p*. But of course someone might fail to see that X and Y do fulfill these conditions, and then (provided he does not himself regard Y as similar to X in the relevant respects) he could without logical absurdity morally condemn X without condemning Y, though we should have to say either that he was ill-informed or that his system of condemnings and condonings was not consistent through and through.

VI

I mentioned a few paragraphs back that in addition to the logical commitments on which I have been laying stress there are moral commitments that might be confused with them and that must be distinguished from them. I shall mention briefly two of these:

1. When I morally condemn actions of kind X I am thereby morally committed to avoiding such actions; and when I morally condemn some particular action I am morally committed to avoiding actions that I regard as similar to it in the relevant respects. We have already seen that to say of someone, "He morally condemns X but does it," is not to say anything *logically* absurd; but the man of whom it is true has done wrong. (Aristotle's remarks about there being situations in which the pressure on a man is so great that pity rather than blame may be in place are doubtless relevant here as qualifying clauses; but I shall not try to amplify that here.)

2. If I condemn some action X and by my words or by other signs wittingly give the impression that my condemnation is to be understood as *moral* condemnation (and there are several ways in which this could be done), then I am morally committed to *either* (a) making good my claim that my condemnation was moral condemnation by going on to condemn whatever I regard as relevantly similar to X, *or* (b) withdrawing my (overt or implied) claim that my condemnation of X was moral condemnation. As far as what I have said about logical commitment is concerned, my failure to condemn what I consider relevantly similar to X will merely *falsify* any claim I may have made to have been condemning X morally. What I am now saying is that if I have made such a claim I am *morally* committed either to see to it that my claim is not so falsified or else to withdraw that claim. There may of course sometimes be good moral reasons why I should refrain from *publicizing* my condemnation of some particular action, or why I should conceal my condemnation of it from some particular person, but that again is a complication I shall not try to discuss here.

A. N. PRIOR

Escapism:
The Logical Basis of Ethics

A SIMPLIFICATION OF DEONTIC LOGIC

In what follows I shall use the ordinary Lukasiewicz symbols for truth functors (N for "not," C for "if," Kpq for "p and q," Apq for "p or q") and modal functors (L for "necessarily," M for "possibly"), supplemented by O for "It is obligatory that . . . ," P for "It is permissible that . . . ," and F for "It is forbidden that. . . ." I shall sometimes read LCpq, "Necessarily if p then q," as "p necessitates q," and MKpq, "Possibly both p and q," as "p is compatible with q"; e.g., CMpCLCpqMKpq may be read as "If p is possible, then if p necessitates q then p is compatible with q," i.e., what is possible at all is compatible with whatever it necessitates.

Using these symbols, a plausible set of postulates for what is now often called "deontic" logic would be the definition (Df. P) Pp = NONp, and the four axioms

O1.OCOpp   O3.COCpqCOpOq
O2.COpPp   O4.CLCpqCOpOq,

all subjoined to some postulate-set sufficient for ordinary modal logic. That is, we define the permissible as that which we are not obliged to refrain from, and we assume that it is obligatory that what is obligatory be done (O1); that what is obligatory is permissible (O2); that, when doing one thing without another is forbidden, then if the first thing is obligatory so is the second (O3—I am reading the antecedent OCpq as its equivalent NPKpNq); that whatever is necessitated by an obligation is itself an obligation (O4).

These, I have suggested, are to be thought of as "subjoined to some postulate-set sufficient for ordinary modal logic." For example, to the postulates for Feys's system T, which consist of ordinary propositional calculus with substitution and detachment, supplemented by the definition (Df. M) Mp = NLNp (may be = need-not not-be), the two axioms

    L1.CLpp (what is necessary is true)

    L2.CLCpqCLpLq (what is necessarily implied by a necessary proposition is necessary),

and the rule (RL) that if a is a law of the system so is La (we may assert as necessary whatever has been laid down as, or found to be, a logical law). Or we might, for our "ordinary modal system," use Gödel's postulates for S4, i.e., the above for T together with the extra axiom

    L3.CLpLLp (what is necessary is necessarily necessary);

or Gödel's for S5, i.e., the above for T together with

    L4.CNLpLNLp (what is not necessary could not be necessary).

We shall later on consider some of the differences it could make to deontic logic to have L3 or L4 among its postulates, but to begin with let us take the weaker system T as our modal basis, and from the propositional calculus draw upon, in particular, the following laws:

1. CCpqCCqrCpr	6. CpCqp
2. CCqrCCpqCpr	7. CCpCqrCCpqCpr
3. CCpqCCqrCCrsCps	8. CpNNp
4. CCpCqrCqCpr	9. CCpqCNqNp
5. Cpp	10. CCpqCpKpq.

The following will serve to illustrate what is provable in this modal system (I select examples that will be useful later):

11. LCpp (5, RL)
12. CLpLCqp (6, RL, L2)
13. CpCLCpqq (L1 p/Cpq, 4)
14. LCpLCpqq (13, RL)
15. CLCpCqrLCCpqCpr (7, RL, L2)
16. CLCpCqrCLCpqLCpr (1, 15, L2)
17. CLCpqLCNqNp (9, RL, L2)
18. CLCpqCNLNpNLNq (3; 17; L2 p/Nq, q/Np; 9 p/LNq, q/LNp)
19. CLCpqCMpMq (18, Df. M)
20. CLCpqLCpKpq (10, RL, L2)
21. CLCpqCMpMKpq (1, 20, 19)
22. CMpCLCpqMKpq (4, 21).

The further deductions that are possible when O1–O4 are added may be illustrated by the following:

23. COpONNp (8, RL, O4)
24. COpNNONNp (1, 23, 8 p/ONNp)
25. COpNPNp (24, Df. P)
26. CLpCOqOp (1, 12, O4)
27. CLpOp (26 q/COpp; 4; O1)
28. CLpPp (1, 27, O2)
29. CNPNpNLNp (9, 28 p/Np)
30. COpNLNp (1, 25, 29)
31. COpMp (30, Df. M).

I shall not try to verbalize all these formulas or all their proofs (any reader who is interested may be invited to do this for himself); but some comment is needed on some of the last few. Proposition 31, asserting that whatever is obligatory is possible ("What I ought I can"), will be generally regarded as reasonable, as will its derivation from 28, asserting that what is unavoidable is permissible. But 28 is itself proved as a simple consequence (by O2, the permissibility of what is obligatory) of 27, asserting that whatever is inevitable is obligatory, a proposition regarded by many with considerable suspicion and uneasiness. But surely this proposition is harmless (this obligation, if it be one, is one that is *always* met, and need not worry us); and better than fussing about its oddity would be to *use* this result to simplify our postulates. For, now that we know that the given postulates yield 27, we know that if we replace O4 by 27 we cannot obtain *more* than before, and that we will not obtain *less* may be shown by deriving O4 by 1 from 27 p/Cpq (i.e., CLCpqOCpq) and O3 (COCpqCOpOq). So let us replace our special deontic postulates O1–O4 by the equivalent set O1, O2, O3, 27.

A much more spectacular simplification, as has been pointed out by Professor Alan Ross Anderson,[1] may be obtained by making our undefined deontic concept not the functor O but an unspecified "sanction" S such that "p is forbidden" may be defined as "p necessitates the sanction," LCpS, and "p is obligatory" as "the omission of p necessitates the sanction," LCNpS. By ordinary modal logic this last is equivalent to LCNSp, "Avoiding the sanction necessitates the performance of p." Using E ("escaping") for NS, we could write this more simply as LCEp, "Escaping necessitates p"; and this definition of O makes the Andersonian simplification very easy to exhibit. (This was pointed out to me by Mr. E. J. Lemmon.) Note that the constants S and E are not mere proposition-forming functors, either monadic ones like N, M, L, O, and P or dyadic like C, K, and A, but are complete propositions, substitutable as they stand for propositional variables in theses. In particular, such substitutions in the modal laws 14, 16, and 12 will immediately yield LCECLCEpp, CLCECpq-CLCEpLCEq, and CLpLCEp, which by Df. O become, respectively, OCOpp. COCpqCOqOq, and CLpOp, i.e., O1, O3, and 27. In words, the definition turns O1 and O3 into

[1] Alan Ross Anderson, *The Formal Analysis of Normative Concepts* (Technical Report No. 2, U.S. Office of Naval Research Contract No. SAR/Nonr-609 16, 1956).

"Escaping necessitates that whatever escaping necessitates be done" and "If escaping necessitates that if p then q, then if escaping necessitates that p it necessitates that q," which are obvious exemplifications of purely modal principles (they would be just as true if "escaping" were replaced by "getting caught," or by "eating cheese"); while 27 is turned into "What is absolutely necessary is necessitated by escaping," which is an obvious exemplification of a well-known and explainable paradox.

We are thus left with O2, COpPp, as our sole special deontic axiom. If Op = LCEp, Pp or NONp would be NLCENp ("Escape does not necessitate refraining from p"), but we obtain an equivalent and shorter result by just defining Pp directly in terms of E as MKEp ("Escape is compatible with p"). This turns O2 into CLCEpMKEp, "If escaping necessitates p then it is compatible with p." This can be false only if escaping is impossible (the impossible, and only the impossible, necessitates everything and is not compatible with anything); so O2 is equivalent in force to the much shorter ME, which may replace it as sole axiom; call it 32 (O2 is then proved from 32 plus 22 p/E, q/p).

THE ADVANTAGES OF A STRONG MODAL LOGIC

That the assertion O2, "Whatever is obligatory is permissible," i.e., nothing is at once obligatory and forbidden, is equivalent to 32, "Escape (from condemnation) is possible," is intuitively evident. What also seems intuitively evident is the equivalence of the following two falsehoods:

1. It is obligatory that only what is obligatory be done.
2. Whatever is not obligatory is forbidden.

We might symbolize (1) as OCpOp, "It is obligatory that if p be done it be obligatory," and (2) as CNOpONp, "If p is not obligatory then it is obligatory to omit it." What both of these formulas express is clearly an excessive rigorism. Now the Andersonian definitions expand these, respectively, to

LCECpLCEp and CNLCEpLCENp, which would be logically equivalent if we had as modal laws the implication:
(a) C(LCpCqLCpq) (CNLCpqLCpNq) and its converse
(b) C(CNLCpqLCpNq) (LCpCqLCpq). But of these, only the second is found in modal systems weaker than S5 (and even the second is only in S4, and not in T). For the matrix

C	1	2	3	4	N	L
1	1	2	3	4	4	1
2	1	1	3	3	3	4
3	1	2	1	2	2	3
4	1	1	1	1	1	4

which verifies all the postulates of S4, falsifies (a) (When p = 1, q = 3, (a) = 3. This assignment of values, we may note, would also verify Mp, i.e., NLNp; so (a) is still falsifiable by this matrix when for p we put a proposition E for which ME is a law). We can, however, prove (a) as well as (b) quite easily in S5, i.e., in the system containing the law L4, CNLpLNLp. For in S5 we have in succession

33. CNqCCpqNp (4, 9)
34. CNLCpqCCpCqLCpqCpNq (1; 33 p/q, q/LCpq; 2)
35. CLNLCpqLCCpCqLCpqCpNq (34, RL, L2)
36. CNLCpqLCCpCqLCpqCpNq (1; L4 p/Cpq; 35)
37. CNLCpqCLCpCqLCpqLCpNq (1; 36; L2)
38. CLCpCqLCpqCNLCpqLCpNq (4, 37).

And, to unwind this reel again, the substitution p/E, q/p in 38 yields CLCECpLCEpCNLCEpLCENp, "If escaping necessitates that p-be-done-only-if-escaping-necessitates-it, then if escaping does not necessitate that p be done it necessitates that it be omitted"; which by Df. O gives us COCpOp-CNOpONp, "If it is obligatory that we do nothing but what we are obliged to do, then what is not obligatory is positively forbidden." That this implication is provable only in S5 does seem to me an argument in favor of that system.

There is at least one other point at which the presence or absence of L4 makes a noticeable difference. To locate this point of difference, we must first digress a little. As Anderson has pointed out, one way of avoiding such paradoxes as that what is inevitable is obligatory (our 27) and what is impossible is forbidden (27 p/NP) is to include the contingency of the act in question (i.e., its being neither necessary nor impossible; or both it and its omission being possible) in the very definitions of the positive notions of obligation, permissibility, and forbiddenness, so that we have, using (O), (P), and (F) for these new notions:

Df. (O): (O)p = KLCEpKMpMNp
Df. (F): (F)p = KLCENpKMpMNp
Df. (P): (P)p = KMKEpKMpMNp.

Given these definitions we can still prove, for example, that whatever is impossible is not permissible, but "not permissible" does not now mean or imply "forbidden"—what is impossible is not permissible, not because it is forbidden, nor because its opposite (i.e., what is necessary) is obligatory, but because it is neither permissible, forbidden, nor obligatory; and its opposite likewise. There are people who find this position attractive, and even those who do not must admit that this is a possible way of using the words "permissible" and so forth.

If, now, we append these definitions to the strong modal system S5, it may be shown that whatever is obligatory, permissible, or forbidden is necessarily so. This depends on the fact that (1) in S5, M = LM and L = LL, and (2) in any ordinary modal system, LKpq = KLpLq, and LKpKqr = KLpKLqLr. So for (P) we have

(P)p = KLCEpKMpMNp (Df. (P))
   = KLLCEpKLMpLMNp (L = LL, M = LM)
   = LKLCEpKMpMNp (KLpKLqLr = LKpKqr)
   = L (P)p (Df. (P)).

The proofs of $(F)p = L(F)p$ and $(O)p = L(O)p$ are similar. It may also be shown that if any of these forms $(P)p$ and so forth are false they are necessarily false. Taking $(P)p$ again as an example, the proof goes thus:

$$N(P)p = NL(P)p \; ((P) = L(P), \text{ proved above})$$
$$= LNL(P)p \; (NL = LNL \text{ in } S_5)$$
$$= LN(P)p \; (L(P) = (P), \text{ as above}).$$

Similarly with $N(O)$ and $N(F)$. Hence $(P)p$, $(F)p$, and $(O)p$ are always either necessary or impossible, never contingent. Hence they can never themselves be permissible, forbidden, or obligatory, for (by the definitions) they could only be any of these if they *were* contingent. That is, we have as laws everything of the form $NXYp$, where X and Y can be (P), (F), or (O)—we have $N(P)(P)p$, $N(P)(O)p$, $N(P)(F)p$, $N(F)(P)p$, and so on.

This result may seem odd, and therefore an argument against S_5; but I do not think it is really so. Remember again that what is, say, "not permissible" (in the present sense of "permissible") may be so for either of two reasons—either because it is forbidden, or because it is not contingent, and so not the sort of thing that can be permissible *or* forbidden. And permissibilities, obligations, and forbiddennesses fall under the second head.

The following is a context in which an appreciable difference is made even by the weaker thesis L_3, $CLpLLp$, characteristic of S_4: A propositional constant logically equivalent to E cannot be defined in an ordinary deontic system with O, P, or F as primitive unless we introduce quantifiers binding propositional variables; but it can be done then. For given such quantifiers we can formulate the proposition $\Pi pCOpp$, "For all p, if p is obligatory it is done"; and it is possible even with the comparatively weak modal basis T, and without appealing to the special axiom ME, to prove in an E-logic that this proposition ΠpCOpp is logically equivalent to the "escape"-clause E. (We escape the sanction if and only if all our obligations are met.) For, using Lukasiewicz' rules Π1 and Π2 for quantifiers, we have in succession

   39. CΠpCOppCOpp (5, Π1)
   40. CΠpCOppCOEE (substitution for free p in 39)
   41. CΠpCOppCLCEEE (40, Df. O)
   42. CLCEECΠpCOppE (4, 41)
   43. LCEE (11)
   44. CΠpCOppE (42, 43).

And conversely

   45. CECLCEpp (L1 p/CEp; 4)
   46. CECOpp (44, Df. O)
   47. CEΠpCOpp (45, Π2).

This means that in an old-style system with O undefined, provided that we had quantifiers, we could introduce E by definition as ΠpCOpp, and we would obtain a system equivalent to an Andersonian one if we had for axioms MΠpCOpp (i.e., ME), CLCΠpCOpppOp and COpLCΠpCOppp (i.e., CLCEpOp and COpLCEp, corresponding to the Andersonian definition Op = LCEp). These last are not a very attractive set of axioms, but they are provable as theorems in any O-system containing, on top of modal logic, the laws

   O4.CLCpqCOpOq   O6.COpMp (= 31)
   O5.OΠpCOpp   O7.COpLOp.

For MΠPCOpp follows directly from O5 and O6, and the others are derivable thus:

   48. COpCLCpqOq (4, O4)
   49. CLCΠpCOpppOp (48 p/ΠpCOpp, q/p; O5)

and thus:

   50. COpCΠpCOppp (5 p/COpp, Π1; 4)
   51. CLOpLCΠpCOppp (50, RL, L2)
   52. COpLCΠpCOppp (1, O7, 50)

O7 is not, however, provable in an Andersonian deontic logic based on T, but only in one based on at least S4; where L3, CLpLLp, gives us CLCEpLLCEp, i.e., COpLOp.

Anderson's suggestion, then, (1) simplifies deontic logic, and (2) suggests new ways of attaching the differences between T, S4, and S5 to intuitive considerations. But it has its own problems, too. The most striking of these is perhaps best exhibited by using Anderson's own form of his logic, with an undefined "sanction" S, and Fp ("p is forbidden") defined as LCpS. From the modal law (present even in T)

53. CLCpqCLCqrLCpr

("What is necessitated by what is necessitated by p, is necessitated by p"), we have by substitution

54. CLCpqCLCqSLCpS,

"What necessarily implies what necessarily implies the sanction, itself necessarily implies the sanction"; or, more briefly, what necessarily implies what is forbidden, is itself forbidden. For example, helping someone who has been robbed with violence is an act that can only occur if the person has been so robbed ("X helps Y who has been robbed" necessarily implies, "Y has been robbed"); but the robbery (being wrong) necessarily implies the sanction; therefore the succor (since it implies robbery) implies the sanction, too, and is also wrong.

We might call this the Paradox of the Good Samaritan. I have heard different solutions offered for it, and have offered different ones myself; but the one I am now most inclined to put forward is what might be called the "existentialist" solution (it was suggested to me by some remarks of Dr. H. P. Rickman, but he is not to be blamed for it as I now give it), namely, that each person should regard deontic logic as applying to those measures he must take to avoid the sanction that threatens *him*. From this point of view a wrong done by someone else simply does not concern "the person whose deontic logic this is" *as* a wrong, i.e., as a thing on account of which the sanction hangs over *him*, but merely, as it were, helps to set the stage on which the acts for which he really is responsible take place. So here we have no LCqS—the robbers' robbery, q, just does not necessitate the Samaritan's sanction S, though it no doubt necessitates another sanction S_1 on which *their* (i.e., the robbers') deontic logic is founded. This "relativization" of deontic logic, making it give the structure common to a multitude of different personal contexts, seems to me entirely unobjectionable.

Another question: Is the Andersonian deontic logic "naturalistic"? We might begin to answer this by noting that we can prove in this system, at least in the forms here considered (other forms are possible with other modal bases [2]), the proposition OE, i.e., that we have an obligation to escape from the sanction. And this at first seems very wonderful. For you know these conversations in which A says, "The obligatory is just whatever is needed to further X," and B says, "But why is furthering X obligatory?" and almost always A has no answer to this one; but here, now, is a man who can *prove* that furthering X, in this case escaping the sanction, is obligatory. When, however, we turn to the proof itself, it is not so impressive. OE is true because it is (by Df. O) just a way of saying LCEE, "Escaping necessarily implies escaping," or "Necessarily if you escape you escape," i.e., our proposition 43, which is proved simply by the substitution p/E in 11, LCpp. Something Moore said long ago—and, we are told, others before him—makes us restless at this point. "Is this, then," we ask, "all that the obligation to escape amounts to—that to escape, we must escape?" And not only this obligation, but all obligation, is somehow made empty now.

[2] Cf. my *Time and Modality* (Oxford: Clarendon Press, 1957), Appendix D.

Really this system is not about ethics at all—it is about the technique of escaping from something you fear, and that is all there is to it.

But this is going further than the formulas warrant. Certainly OE is a tautology (in the sense in which LCpp is a tautology), but this could be not because "obligation" means too little, but because "escaping" means too much, for it to be anything else. For remember the other theorem (44 and 47) that E is equivalent to ΠpCOpp, i.e., that "escaping" is what occurs if and only if we meet *all* our obligations. "Escaping" is thus not merely not suffering but not *deserving* any penalty; the postulated "sanction" is some completely effective one, in that wrongdoing by definition *necessitates* it; and how this is secured the symbols do not say, but it could be done as well by spiritualizing the sanction as by debasing the "desert" and "obligation" involved. The sanction to be escaped can be, if we like, simply failure to "be perfect." Or it can be—for, though this is not necessitated by the system, it is not excluded either—being caught breaking that safe. (If this is our S, breaking the safe is not Andersonianly forbidden so long as it can be done without being caught.) So we again encounter the picture of deontic logic as "giving the structure common to a multitude of different personal contents"; we are now seeing *how* different the personal contents can be.

We may learn also, from what has just been said, that the Andersonian simplification of deontic logic involves a discovery as well as a dodge—the discovery, namely, that the logic, the pure structure, of "being perfect" is the same as the pure structure of escaping from what we fear, so that the same calculus can be turned indifferently to the one use or the other. This is worth coming to know—for there is a beauty in such parallelisms which it is a pleasure to contemplate— even if it leaves us none the wiser as to precisely what we ought to do.

GILBERT RYLE

On Forgetting the Difference
between Right and Wrong

"Don't you know the difference between right and wrong?"
"Well, I did learn it once, but I have forgotten it." This is a
ridiculous thing to say. But why is it ridiculous? We forget
lots of things, including lots of important things, that we used
to know. So what is the absurdity in the idea of a person's forgetting the difference between right and wrong?

I think the question worthy of discussion, if only because the
epistemological wheels on which ethical theories are made
to run are apt to be wooden and uncircular.

Only one philosopher, so far as I know, has discussed my
question. Aristotle does so very briefly in the *Nicomachean
Ethics* 1100^b 17 and 1140^b 29.

First let us get rid of two possible misconstructions of my
question.

In speaking of a person's knowing or not knowing the difference between right and wrong, I shall not be speaking of
him as knowing or not knowing the solutions to philosophers'
conceptual questions like, "What are the definitions of Rightness and Wrongness, respectively?" A properly brought up

child knows the difference between right and wrong, for all that he has never heard an argument from Kant or Thrasymachus and would not have understood their definitions if he had. Anyhow, there is no absurdity in the idea of philosophy student's having forgotten some ethical definitions or analyses that he had once known. He would not thereby cease to know the difference between right and wrong.

Next, the assertion that it is absurd to say that a person might forget the difference between right and wrong could be misconstrued as the ascription to our knowledge of right and wrong of an inspiring kind of indelibility, perhaps a Heaven-hinting innateness or a trailing cloud of glory. No such edifying moral can be looked for. If it is absurd to say that one has forgotten the difference, it is also absurd to say that one recollects it. If it is absurd to say that one's knowledge of the difference between right and wrong might, like one's Latin, get rusty, then it is also absurd to say that it actually remains, like one's English, unrusty.

1. It might be suggested that there is a quite simple reason why we cannot forget the difference between right and wrong, namely, that daily life gives us constant reminders of it. Somewhat as, throughout December, Christmas carols, Christmas cards, and butchers' shops constantly remind us of the imminence of Christmas Day, so the daily procession of duties to be done and derelictions to be apologized for keeps us constantly in mind of the difference between right and wrong. But this explanation will not do. A very forgetful person remains unreminded in the midst of reminders. Even the knot in his handkerchief does not remind him of anything. Moreover, a man might happen to sojourn in a part of the world where there were no reminders of Christmas. If this were all, then the maker of the paradoxical remark might just be in the rare position of being unusually forgetful or unusually unexposed to obligations; and then his remark would be not ridiculous but only hard to credit. Forgetting the difference be-

tween right and wrong would then be merely a rare thing, like forgetting one's own name.

This suggested explanation is a causal hypothesis. It offers to tell what makes people very unlikely to forget the difference between right and wrong. It therefore assumes that there is such a thing as forgetting this difference. But our question is, rather, "Why is there no such thing? Why will 'forget' and 'be reminded of' not to go with 'the difference between right and wrong'?"

2. A better, though still inadequate, explanation would be this. Knowing the difference between right and wrong is of a piece not with remembering particular matters of fact, like names, dates, and engagements, but with knowing how to do things, knowing the way from place to place, knowing Latin, and knowing the rules of the road in one's own country. Such things do not slip our memories, nor are knots tied in our handkerchiefs to keep us in mind of them. Knowledge here is mastery of techniques rather than mere possession of information; it is a capacity that can improve or decline, but cannot just come in and go out. We acquire such knowledge not just from being told things, but from being trained to do things. The knowledge is not imparted but inculcated. It is a second nature, and therefore not evanescent. Now our knowledge of the difference between right and wrong certainly is in many important respects much more like a mastery than like the retention of a piece of information. It is, for instance, inculcated by upbringing rather than imparted by dictation. It is not a set of things memorized and is not, consequently, the sort of knowledge of which shortness of memory is the natural enemy.

Nonetheless, there is such a thing as forgetting much or all of one's Latin. With desuetude, one does become rustier and rustier, until one has totally forgotten it. We know what we have to do to keep up our Latin, our geometry, or our tennis, namely, to give ourselves regular practice. Just here is one place where the analogy breaks down between knowing the difference between right and wrong and having mastery of a science or a craft. One's knowledge of the difference between right and wrong does not get rusty; we do not keep up our honesty by giving ourselves regular exercises in it. Nor do we excuse a malicious action by saying that we have recently been short of practice in fair-mindedness and generosity. Virtues are not proficiencies. The notion of being out of practice, which is appropriate to skills, is inappropriate to virtues.

Aristotle's explanation of the fact that there is no such thing as forgetting the difference between right and wrong seems to be that moral dispositions are, from constant exercise, much more abiding things than even our masteries of sciences and crafts. In the latter there is forgetting, though only gradual forgetting; in the former there happens to be none. But the difference does not seem to be just a difference in degree, or even just a difference between a small magnitude and zero. Nor is it just a matter of anthropological fact that our knowledge of the difference between right and wrong never decays. The notion of decay does not fit.

En passant, when I argue that we do not impose moral exercises upon ourselves in order to prevent our knowledge of the difference between right and wrong from rusting, since the notion of rusting does not belong, I am not denying that we can or should drill ourselves into good habits and out of bad ones. I am only denying that such self-disciplining is to be assimilated to the exercises by which we prevent our Latin or our tennis from getting rusty. The object of moral drills is not to save us from forgetting the difference between right and wrong, but to stiffen us against doing what we know to be wrong.

Neither, to make the obverse point, am I denying that moral deterioration occurs. People often do get more callous, less public-spirited, meaner, lazier, and shiftier. What I am denying is that such deteriorations are to be assimilated to declines in expertness, i.e., to getting rusty.

3. A third explanation would be this. Since virtues are not skills, that is, since to be unselfish or patient is not to be good *at* doing anything, perhaps virtues should be classed rather with tastes and preferences, and particularly with educated tastes and cultivated preferences. As the music lover had once to learn to appreciate music, and the bridge player had to learn both to play and to enjoy playing bridge, so the honest man had to be taught or trained to dislike deception, and the charitable man had to be taught or trained to want to relieve distress. Doubtless, as some people take to music from the start as a duck takes to water, so some people are naturally more prone than others to be frank and sympathetic. But to be honest or charitable on principle, even against the impulses of the moment, involves knowing the difference between right and wrong—much as, unlike the mere relishing of one piece of music more than another, appreciating the superiority of the one piece over the other involves knowing their relative merits and demerits. Taste is educated preference, preference for recognized superiorities. To be able to recognize superiorities is to know the difference between good and bad.

Now likings, whether natural or cultivated, can be lost. Most grown-ups have lost the enthusiasm for playing hide-and-seek, and some cease to enjoy tobacco and poetry. There can also be deteriorations in taste. A person who once had appreciated the excellences of Jane Austen might become so coarsened in palate as to cease to recognize or relish them.

It is relevant to my problem that we do not call such losses or deteriorations "forgetting." Perhaps the absurdity in speaking of someone's forgetting the difference between right and wrong is of a piece with the absurdity in speaking of someone who has lost the taste for poetry as having forgotten the difference between good and bad poetry.

When a person has an educated taste, he can speak of himself as having learned or been taught not only to recognize the differences between, say, good and bad singing or good and bad tennis strokes, but also to appreciate, i.e., to like, admire, and try for the good and to dislike, despise, and avoid the bad. Knowing, in this region, goes hand in hand with approving and disapproving, relishing and disrelishing, admiring and despising, pursuing and avoiding. Indeed, their connection seems even closer than mere hand-in-hand concomitance. There seems to be a sort of incongruity in the idea of a person's knowing the difference between good and bad wine or poetry, while not caring a whit more for the one than for the other; of his appreciating without being appreciative of excellences. When we read, "We needs must love the highest when we see it," we incline to say, "Of course. We should not be seeing it if we were not loving it. The 'needs must' is a conceptual one. At least in this field, the partitions are down between the Faculties of Cognition, Conation, and Feeling."

Now whether this inclination is justified or not, it exists just as much in our thinking about the knowledge of right and wrong. Here, too, there seems to be an incongruity in the idea of a person's knowing that something wrong had been done, but still not disapproving of it or being ashamed of it; of his knowing that something would be the wrong thing for him to do, but still not scrupling to do it. We hanker to say that, if he has no scruples at all in doing the thing, then he cannot know that it is wrong, but only, perhaps, that it is "wrong," i.e., what other people call "wrong."

Socrates used to ask the important question, "Can Virtue be taught?" It puzzled him, very properly, that if virtue can be taught there exist no pundits in courage, abstinence, or justice. If we, too, think that knowledge of the difference between right and wrong is knowledge, ought we not to be puzzled that universities and technical colleges do not give

courses in industriousness, fair-mindedness, and loyalty? But
the moment such a suggestion is made, we realize that the non-
existence of pundits and colleges of the virtues is not a lamen-
table lacuna in our society. It would be silly to try to provide
such instruction; silly, since knowledge of the difference between right and wrong is not the sort of thing that such instruction could bestow. We continue to think that children
have to be taught the difference between right and wrong, but
we know in our bones that this teaching is not a species of
either factual or technical instruction. What sort of teaching,
then, is the teaching of the difference between right and
wrong? What sort of learning is the learning of this difference?
What kind of knowing is the knowing of it? Maybe we can
approach an answer to these questions by considering the
teaching and learning of tastes.

A person who has received technical instruction in tennis,
music, or landscape gardening may, but may not, owe to his
instructor a second debt of gratitude for having taught him
also to enjoy these things. A person who has learned from a
geographer and a botanist the special features of the Lake
District may have been inspired by Wordsworth also to love
this district for these features. As one gets to know a person
better, one may learn to respect or admire him. Learning to
enjoy, to love, or to admire is not acquiring a skill or a parcel
of information. Nonetheless it *is* learning. There is a difference between a mere change-over from disliking rice pud-
ding to liking it, and learning to appreciate wines, poems, or
people for their excellences. Learning to appreciate requires
some studiousness, judiciousness, and acuteness. The judge
has reasons to give for his likings, his verdicts, and his choices.

True, the special notions of *lessons, instruction, coaching,
examinations, laboratories, courses, manuals,* and the like are
no part of the idea of learning to enjoy or learning to admire.
Even if Wordsworth really does teach us to love the Lake
District, he does not merit or need a professor's chair. But this

is only to say again that admiring, enjoying, and loving are not efficiencies or equipments. The notions of *learning, studying, teaching,* and *knowing* are ampler notions than our academic epistemologies have acknowleged. They are hospitable enough to house under their roofs notions like those of *inspiring, kindling,* and *infecting.*

It will be objected, I expect, that what is called "learning to enjoy" or "being taught to admire" is really always two processes, namely, (1) coming to know some things, and (2) as an effect of coming to know them, coming to like or admire. An emotional condition, disposition, or attitude is caused by a cognitive act or disposition. As the rolling of the ship makes me feel sick, so discovering a person's characteristics makes me experience feelings of admiration toward him. So, presumably, as certain nostrums save me from feeling sick when the ship rolls, certain other nostrums might save me from admiring a person when I have discovered what a stanch friend he is. Alternatively, if this sounds too ridiculous, then a peculiarly intimate kind of causal connection has to be invoked in order to represent the connection between knowing and admiring as still a causal one, and yet as one that is exempt from preventions.

If we ask what the supposedly antecedent process of coming to know consists in, we are likely to be told that it consists in coming to be equipped with some information or/and coming to be relatively efficient at doing certain sorts of things, *plus*, perhaps, coming to be able and ready to explain, instruct, criticize, and so forth. These are not effects of coming to know; they are concrete examples of what coming to know is coming to. But why not add that sometimes coming to know *is*, also, *inter alia*, coming to admire or enjoy? If making a skillful tennis stroke or a skillful translation is doing something that one has learned to do, i.e., is an exercise and not an effect of knowledge, why may not admiring a person for his stanchness be, in a partly similar way, an example and not an aftereffect

of what our study of his character has taught us? The reply
that what is learned must be either a piece of information or
a technique begs the question, since the question is, in part,
"Why must it be either one or the other?"

How does all this apply to our knowledge of the difference
between right and wrong? We are unwilling to allow that a
person has learned this difference who does not, for instance,
care a bit whether he breaks a promise or keeps it, and is quite
indifferent whether someone else is cruel or kind. This *caring* is not a special feeling; it covers a variety of feelings, like
those that go with being shocked, ashamed, indignant, admiring, emulous, disgusted, and enthusiastic; but it also covers
a variety of actions, as well as readinesses and pronenesses to
do things, like apologizing, recompensing, scolding, praising,
persevering, praying, confessing, and making good resolutions.
Now, if we consider what in detail a person who has learned
the difference between right and wrong has learned, we do not
naturally draw a line between some things, namely, what he
has learned to say and do, and other things, namely, what he
has learned to feel, and relegate the latter to the class of mere
aftereffects of his learning to say and do the proper things. In
thinking about his conscience or his sense of duty, we do not
naturally fence off his qualms from his acts of reparation; his
pangs from his confessings or his resolvings; his prick-
ings from his perseverings. *Because* he has learned the
difference between right and wrong, he both makes reparations
and feels contrite; and the "because" is the same noncausal
"because." Certainly his feeling contrite is not an exercise of
a technique or the giving of a piece of information; but the
same is true, though for different reasons, of his making reparations, persevering, reproaching, resolving, and keeping appoint-
ments. All are marks, though different sorts of marks, of his
knowing the difference between right and wrong; all show,
though in different ways, that he has principles, and what these
principles are; any one of them is one of the many sorts of

things that we have in mind when we say of him that he has a sense of duty.

Now we can begin to see why it is ridiculous to say that one has forgotten the difference between right and wrong. To have been taught the difference is to have been brought to appreciate the difference, and this appreciation is not just a competence to label correctly or just a capacity to do things efficiently. It includes an inculcated caring, a habit of taking certain sorts of things seriously.

A person who used to care may, indeed, cease to care or to care so much. But ceasing to care is not forgetting, any more than ceasing to believe something or to mistrust someone is forgetting. "Forget" is reserved, apparently, mainly for the nonretention of information and the loss of skills through desuetude, though it is also used for ceasing to notice things, e.g., for the oblivion brought by sleep or distractions.

This use of "forget" for the loss of information and technical abilities, and its nonuse for cessations of caring, may go with another difference. If I have ceased to enjoy bridge, or come to admire Picasso, then I have changed. But, if I have forgotten a date or become rusty in my Latin, I do not think of this as a change in *me*, but rather as a diminution of my equipment. In the same way, a person who becomes less or more conscientious is a somewhat changed person, not a person with an enlarged or diminished stock of anything. In a testimonial both personal qualities and equipment need to be mentioned, but the equipment is not mentioned among the personal qualities.

So far I have been pressing some analogies between things like tastes and pastimes on the one hand and virtues on the other; I have concentrated on ways in which the notions of *learning, teaching,* and *knowing* lock in with notions of *caring,* i.e., *enjoying, admiring, despising, trying, avoiding,* and so forth; and I have tried to show how, in these connections, they detach themselves from the notion of *forgetting*. But we must not push assimilation to the point of identification.

The man who knows the difference between good and bad tennis strokes, and applauds or tries for the good ones and pities or avoids the bad ones, is something of a specialist. The man who appreciates wines is something of a connoisseur. They have acquired special technical abilities and, therewith, special enjoyments. We others may envy them for both. But knowledge of the difference between right and wrong is common knowledge, and it is not mastery of a technique. There is nothing in particular that the honest man knows, ex officio, how to do. He is not, ex officio, even a bit of an expert at anything. Nor is his life enriched by some extra relishes. He possesses nothing for us to envy.

Often, though not always, we study to become relatively good at things, e.g., games, fine arts, and recreations, because we either enjoy them from the start or anyhow expect to get pleasure from them in the end. Our elders coerce us into learning to swim, largely because they think that we shall miss a lot of pleasure afterward if we do not learn to swim, or to swim well. But this is nothing like the reason or reasons for which elders train the young to be honest. The truth lover has no treats to match against those of the music lover. A sense of duty is not an esthetic sensibility; nor is the passion for righteousness indulged as the passion for bridge or birdwatching is indulged. It is not addiction to a sport or hobby. Certainly there are activities, like most work, in which, although technical excellence pleases and bad craftsmanship displeases, still the jobs are not done or even done well only for pleasure's sake. But the honest or charitable man has not, ex officio, any particular job to do, much less to be proud of doing well rather than botching. Knowing the difference between right and wrong is not identical with knowing the difference between good and bad work, even though they resemble one another in the fact that ceasing to care how one does one's job, like ceasing to care what one does, is not a case of forgetting.

One more reinsurance. I have claimed to detect an incongruity, and the same sort of incongruity, in the idea of a man's knowing the difference between right and wrong but not caring a bit whether he lies, say, or tells the truth; in the idea of a man's recognizing, without being appreciative of, the excellences of Jane Austen; and in the idea of a craftsman's knowing the difference between good and bad workmanship without taking any pride in his own good work or feeling any contempt for the bad work of others. I may seem to have equated this knowing with having learned to take seriously. But there is a trap here.

I may be a bit shocked and indignant at an exhibition of unfairness, while you are much shocked and highly indignant. I care a bit about it, and you care much more. But this does not involve that you know more differences between right and wrong than I do, if this makes any sense, or that you know the difference better, if this makes any sense. Similarly, a specimen of Shakespeare's literary genius may please me while it thrills you. We appreciate the same excellence, though we are unequally appreciative of it. So even if, in some domains, to teach is, *inter alia*, to kindle, still we do not think of what is taught as varying in magnitude with the heat of the fire. The match is the same, but the fuels are different.

One last point. In most fields instructors can misinstruct. I may be taught that the Battle of Hastings was fought in 1077, and I may be taught to grip fiercely my billiard cue and my steering wheel. While I retain faith in my instructor, I shall still claim to know the date of the battle and to know how to control the cue and the steering wheel; but, when I have learned better, I shall agree that I had not formerly known the date of the battle or how to control the cue or the wheel. I have to unlearn what I was originally taught.

There is no difficulty in conceiving of misinstruction in the particular articles of codes of etiquette. A boy might well be trained to remain respectfully hatted in a lady's drawing room and punctiliously to end his letters to tradesmen with "Yours sincerely." Nor is there much difficulty in conceiving of misinstruction in some of the bylaws of morality. Some people used scrupulously to pay all their gambling debts before paying off any of their debts to servants and tradesmen. Their consciences had been educated to insist on this priority.

But there is a difficulty in conceiving of a person's being taught to be selfish, deceitful, cruel, and lazy on principle; to be morally shocked at exhibitions of fair-mindedness; or scrupulously to make reparations for his backslidings into unselfishness. The notion of moral noneducation is familiar enough, but the notion of moral miseducation has a smell of absurdity. There is a whiff of the same smell of absurdity in the notion of the would-be connoisseur of wines or engravings being mistaught, taught, that is, to relish wines for their immaturity or to admire engravings for their smudginesses. However, the smell of absurdity is less strong here. The Albert Memorial does seem to have been admired for its architectural badnesses.

The oddness, if it exists, in the idea of moral miseducation might be one source of the strength of the notion of The Moral Law. But to follow up this train of thought would seduce me into talking Ethics.

MARCUS G. SINGER

Moral Rules and Principles

It has generally been recognized that there is a distinction, of some importance, between moral rules and moral principles. Yet the distinction has not generally received explicit formulation, and there is no general agreement on just what it is. These terms tend to be used in different ways, and consequently the distinction between them has been drawn at different places. I shall make no attempt, however, to take account of all uses of these terms. Different purposes require different classifications and hence different distinctions. I shall use these terms in such a way that moral principles are more general, pervasive, and fundamental than moral rules, and in some sense their sources or grounds. It is in accordance with this usage that we sometimes speak of the principle underlying a certain rule, determining its scope and justifying exceptions to it. And this usage certainly has respectable precedents. It is, for one thing, basic in the utilitarian tradition, which distinguishes the principle of utility from the moral rules that it sanctions or authorizes. A distinction along these lines is stated explicitly by Whewell, who speaks of moral principles as the "fundamental maxims or rules, the basis of other rules," and says that "in order . . . to establish

160

and apply moral rules, we must state the moral principles
which are the foundation of such rules." [1] The sort of distinction I have in mind, furthermore, corresponds very closely
to that between *legal* rules and *legal* principles which has been
formulated by Roscoe Pound: "Legal principles . . . are
made use of to supply new rules, to intercept old ones, to meet
new situations, to measure the scope and application of rules
and standards and to reconcile them when they conflict or
overlap. . . ." [2] The distinctions embodied in the traditions
on which I have just reported, however, are not *exactly* like
the one to be set forth here, and I am not prepared to accept,
as *principles*, those laid down, for example, by Whewell, or
even the principle of utility.[3]

[1] William Whewell, *The Elements of Morality* (3rd ed.; London:
John W. Parker & Son, 1854), Bk. II, chap. iv, p. 117.

[2] Roscoe Pound, *An Introduction to the Philosophy of Law* (New
Haven: Yale University Press, 1922), p. 116. Cf. G. W. Paton, *A Text-
book of Jurisprudence* (2nd ed.; Oxford: Clarendon Press, 1951), p.
176; and John Dickinson, *Administrative Justice and the Supremacy
of Law* (Cambridge, Mass.: Harvard University Press, 1927), pp. 128 ff.

[3] Some other conceptions of moral principles that have recently been
presented may be worth mentioning. K. Baier, for example, in "Decisions and Descriptions," *Mind*, N.S. LX (April, 1951), 199, says:
"Moral principles and moral laws differ from moral rules in that the
former need not be recognized. . . . A moral law or principle becomes
a moral rule by becoming recognized." This seems to me no more than
verbal legislation, without much chance of passing. P. H. Nowell-
Smith, *Ethics* (London: Penguin Books, 1954), regards a moral principle as a "disposition to choose," and speaks of adopting, changing,
and choosing to change one's moral principles (pp. 306–14). I know
of no sense in which a principle can be adopted, and this is reinforced
by the consideration that it is "logically odd" to speak of someone's
adopting different motives or dispositions. (Notice that to "choose to
change one's moral principles" would, on this view, be to "choose to
change one's dispositions to choose.") So I regard this as just another
instance of verbal legislation. This is not to imply that there is *nothing*
to be said for these ways of defining moral principles; it implies that
there is very little. For a further discussion of moral principles, see the
symposium, "When Is a Principle a Moral Principle?" by P. R. Foot
and J. Harrison, in *Belief and Will* (Aristotelian Society Supplementary
Vol. XXVIII) (London: Harrison & Sons, 1954), pp. 95–134. The

But my object in this essay is not simply to distinguish between moral rules and principles. What I hope to show is how moral principles (especially the two that I shall shortly mention) are involved in the justification or establishment of moral rules, and this will involve a further distinction between different kinds of moral rules. My discussion of these matters, furthermore, is intended to have some relevance to questions about the notion of moral justification, the solution of moral problems, and the theory of ethical relativism.

Though some examples of moral principles will be presented later, there are two principles so fundamental in what follows that they should be mentioned here. The first is the principle or line of argument that underlies the use of such familiar questions as "What would happen if everyone did that?" and which I propose to call "the generalization argument": "If the consequences of everyone's acting in a certain way would be disastrous (or undesirable), then no one has the right to act in that way." (This can also be stated in the form: "If the consequences of everyone's acting in a certain way would be undesirable, then it would be wrong for anyone to act in that way," or simply "then it is generally wrong to act in that way.") Closely connected with the generalization argument —indeed, presupposed in its application—is another principle, which I shall call "the generalization *principle*" (though it has traditionally been known as the principle of justice or impartiality): "What is right for one person must be right for any similar person in similar circumstances." It is important to realize that these principles can be stated in alternative ways. For example, the generalization principle can be stated in the form: "If not everyone has the right to act in a

---

basic ambiguity in the term "principle," from which these varying views derive ("principle" is often used in the sense of "motive," and was originally used in the sense of "source" or "origin"), is well brought out by Whewell, *The Elements of Morality*, Bk. II, chap. iv, p. 117.

certain way, then no one has the right to act in that way *without a reason or justification*." Thus the generalization argument can be stated in the form: "If the consequences of everyone's acting in a certain way would be undesirable, then no one has the right to act in that way *without a reason or justification*."

These principles are certainly in need of further elucidation. Yet I shall not try to defend or explain them here (and my excuse must be that I have attempted this elsewhere [4]). Instead, I shall try to apply them. On the theory that the best defense is a good offense, this may well be a sort of defense. For what I shall try to show about the generalization argument is that it serves to generate and establish moral rules and is also involved in determining the range of their application, and that, in cases in which rules conflict, it serves as the principle for deciding or mediating between them.

But first let us consider the nature of moral rules.

I

There are certain kinds of action or courses of conduct that are generally prudent or generally imprudent. It is, for example, generally imprudent to climb very high on a rickety ladder, especially if the rungs happen to be slippery. It follows that there are certain rules, called rules (or maxims) of prudence, to serve as guides to judgment, which state that certain kinds of actions are generally prudent or imprudent. Similarly,

---

[4] "Generalization in Ethics," *Mind*, N.S. LXIV (July, 1955), 361–75. The basic question about the generalization principle is how to determine which persons or circumstances are to be regarded as similar, or, to put it another way, how to determine which similarities between persons or circumstances, out of the many that exist, are morally relevant. My answer, briefly, is that this is determined by the reasons advanced for regarding an act as right, or for regarding a certain case as an exception to a rule, since a reason must always have an application to a class of cases. But there are many other considerations to be kept in mind.

there are certain kinds of actions that are generally right or generally wrong, such as being kind to people, or depriving them of their rightful possessions. If an act is of a kind that is generally right or generally wrong, then it is governed by a moral rule. For a moral rule, as I shall understand the term, is simply a proposition to the effect that a certain kind of action is generally right or generally wrong. Any action of a kind that is generally wrong (or right) may reasonably be presumed to be wrong (or right), and, in the absence of any evidence to the contrary, is wrong (or right). Thus, while it is merely foolish to go against a rule of prudence without a good reason, it is immoral to violate or act contrary to a moral rule without a good reason. An act that violates a moral rule, or appears to do so, requires justification.

The term "right" may be used in either a permissive (weak) sense or a mandatory (strong) sense. In the mandatory sense, to say that an act is right is to say that it is wrong not to do it, and hence to say that it is a duty to do it or that it ought to be done. In the permissive sense, to say that an act is right is not to say that it is wrong not to do it. In this sense "a right act" seems to mean no more than one that is not wrong, or one that the agent has a right to do or not to do as he pleases. (Of course, "right act" may also be used in the sense of a heroic deed, or one that goes beyond what is required. But this sense is not covered by rules.) Now a moral rule can prohibit, require, or permit a certain kind of action (either directly or indirectly). If a certain kind of action is prohibited by a rule, then actions of that kind are generally wrong; if it is required, then it is generally wrong not to do an act of that kind; and, if it is permitted, then actions of that kind are generally not wrong. This last point should take account of the objection that might be felt to speaking of a rule as a proposition. For I am speaking here of moral rules, not of the rules of chess or baseball, which have quite a different character. Moral rules do not define a game.

What I wish to emphasize here is that moral rules state what is right or wrong *usually*, or *for the most part*, though they may not be, and ordinarily are not, stated with this qualification. As examples of moral rules we may take the rules that stealing is wrong, that it is wrong to deceive people, and that everyone ought to keep his promises. The differences of verbal expression are irrelevant. These rules must all be understood with the qualification "generally," or "usually." It is not *always* wrong to lie; it is generally wrong. Similarly, it is not always right to keep a promise; it is generally right; and there are cases in which it is not only justifiable to break a promise, but wrong not to. To say that some kind of action is generally wrong is equivalent to saying that any action of that kind is wrong unless there is a reason to the contrary. (This obviously provides another way of defining moral rules.) To say that a certain kind of action is always wrong would be to say that an action of that kind would be wrong under any and all circumstances or conditions. And, as Mill has pointed out, "It is not the fault of any creed, but of the complicated nature of human affairs, that rules of conduct cannot be so framed as to require no exceptions, and that hardly any kind of action can safely be laid down as either always obligatory or always condemnable." [5] That moral rules require the qualification "generally" is shown by the fact of conflicting claims or obligations. Cases arise in which rules conflict; even if they did not arise in fact they could always be constructed.[6] An action of a kind that is generally wrong and also of a kind that

[5] J. S. Mill, *Utilitarianism* (Everyman's Library ed.; New York: E. P. Dutton & Co., 1910), chap. ii, p. 23.

[6] One famous attempt to deny the possibility of a conflict of rules, or, to use the traditional terminology, a conflict of duties, was made by Kant. But in this case the denial is more apparent than real. For, though Kant denied the possibility of a conflict of duties, he did not deny, but rather affirmed, the possibility of conflicting *grounds of obligation*. See the Introduction to *The Metaphysic of Morals*, in T. K. Abbott (trans.), *Kant's Theory of Ethics* (6th ed.; London: Longman's, Green & Co., 1909), p. 280.

is generally right would be a case of this sort (for actions can be described in different ways). Accordingly, under some circumstances it may be right, or even a duty, to break a promise, tell a lie, or take something that belongs to another without his permission.

There are, of course, other ways of defining moral rules, and it may be possible so to analyze them as to remove all possibility of a conflict between them. One could do this, perhaps, by incorporating explicitly into the statement of a given rule the conditions generally understood to govern its application, and by repeating this process for the rule that, apart from this procedure, would be taken as conflicting with it. This, at any rate, is a procedure that has recently been recommended, and it is well worth examining.

> Our moral rules . . . appear to conflict . . . only because we mistakenly try to analyze them in terms of unconditional rather than conditional statements. When they are regarded as concealed conditional statements, an adequate analysis of the conditions will always remove the possibility of conflict. . . . The rule that a person ought to speak the truth means, among other things, that if a person is asked a question about a matter of fact, if he knows the answer and can give an answer, and *if giving a correct answer would not cause pain or injury to another person*, then he ought to give a correct answer. On the other hand, the rule that a person ought not to cause pain or injury to anyone unnecessarily, means, among other things, that if a person is asked a question about a matter of fact, if he knows the answer and can give the answer, and *if giving a correct answer would cause pain or injury to another person or persons without bringing any benefit to anyone else*, then he ought to give an incorrect answer. If these two rules are analyzed in this way, they do not conflict. . . .[7]

[7] W. J. Rees, "Moral Rules and the Analysis of 'Ought,' " *Philosophical Review*, LXII (January, 1953), 27 (italics added). Cf. the same author's "The General Nature of a Moral Duty," *Philosophy*, XXVIII (January, 1953), 41–57. Other recent discussions of moral rules which I regard as of great interest and importance are: John Rawls, "Two Concepts of Rules," *Philosophical Review*, LXIV (January, 1955), 3–32; and K. Baier, "The Point of View of Morality," *Australasian Journal of Philosophy*, XXXII (August, 1954), 104–35.

Now it may be granted that, "if these two rules are analyzed in this way, they do not conflict," but then neither do they settle anything. For this sort of analysis removes the possibility of conflict between these rules at the expense of creating a class of situations to which they are inapplicable. Suppose A is asked a question about a matter of fact by B and that A knows the answer and can give the answer, and suppose further that if A gives a correct answer C will be injured but B (or perhaps D) will benefit. It is clear that to such a case neither of these rules, analyzed in this way, is applicable, whereas, on what I would regard as the ordinary understanding of them, they are applicable but conflicting. And this class of cases is not a small one. For it is usually the case that giving a correct answer to a question will bring *some* benefit to the person who asked the question—at least he will find out what he wants to know. Thus it is questionable whether this sort of analysis is advantageous, for the question of what ought to be done in such a situation remains. On the one analysis it arises out of a conflict of rules; on the other it arises because of the inapplicability of these rules.

But it is not just a matter of the relative advantages of two competing modes of analysis. For the procedure I am examining seems to me to be mainly *ad hoc*; once a conflict between two rules has been brought out, one can proceed to state them in such a way as to remove it, though with the consequence already mentioned. Though it has been shown that the two rules considered do not conflict, it has not been shown that it is impossible for these rules to conflict with *any other*. One difficulty here is whether it is possible to state explicitly *all* the conditions generally understood to govern the application of a rule. This is not just a pedantic objection. For note the important proviso: "among other things." The statements given do not *exhaust* the meaning of these rules. (And what would a full statement of their meaning look like?) So consider the rule that promises ought to be kept, and suppose that

A has promised B to keep a certain secret, that is to say, never to give the answer to a certain question. Suppose, furthermore, that C asks A the answer to this question. Giving the answer to this question may not cause pain or injury to another person, but it would be the breaking of a promise, and would thus conflict with another rule. Of course, that giving the answer to a certain question would break a promise creates the presumption that it would cause pain or injury to another person, namely, the person to whom the promise was made. But then the important condition of the rule that a person ought to speak the truth, namely, "if giving a correct answer would not cause pain or injury to another person," really amounts to: "if giving a correct answer would not conflict with some other rule." A similar point applies to the second rule, the rule that a person ought not to cause pain or injury to anyone else unnecessarily. The important proviso in the statement of this rule is "without bringing any benefit to anyone else." This seems to me to make the condition in which it occurs equivalent to: "if giving a correct answer would cause pain or injury to another person or persons *without conflicting with some other rule*"; or, to put it another way, "then he ought to give an incorrect answer, *unless giving an incorrect answer would conflict with some other rule*." Thus not all possibilities of conflict have been eliminated.

It may be possible to analyze the rule to keep promises, along the lines indicated, in such a way as to eliminate the conflict between it and the rule to tell the truth. But, for reasons already given, this procedure would be *ad hoc*, and, after the analysis is given, another case can be constructed. Furthermore, if my first point is sound, this analysis would create a large class of situations to which the rule would be inapplicable. I do not deny that the suggestion I have been considering is illuminating for *some* purposes, and the space I have devoted to it should be an indication of its importance. If nothing else, my objections to it should help to clarify the conception of moral rules that I have been advocating. I take the existence of conflicting claims or obligations to be a fact of the moral life, as obvious as that there are conflicts of interests and desires. It is not something to be deduced, but something from which we start, for it is the main source of moral problems. Now any analysis that denies the existence of conflicting claims or obligations must be wrong, and the mode of analysis that I have been examining can avoid this consequence only at the expense of severing all connection between moral rules and moral obligations.

II

So far I have been discussing moral rules, and have said little about how they differ from moral principles. A moral rule states that a certain kind of action is generally wrong (or obligatory), and leaves open the possibility that an act of that kind may be justifiable. Thus moral rules do not hold in all circumstances; they are not invariant; in a useful legal phrase, they are "defeasible." A moral principle, however, states that a certain kind of action (or, in some cases, a certain kind of rule) is always wrong (or obligatory), and does not leave open the possibility of justifying an action of that kind. Moral principles hold in all circumstances and allow of no exceptions; they are invariant with respect to every moral judgment and every moral situation. They are thus "indefeasible." It should be clear that such principles are bound to be somewhat more abstract than moral rules, though they are not necessarily less definite.

The principle of a rule can be thought of as analogous to the intent of a piece of legislation, which is the purpose it was designed to achieve, and hence the reason for its existence. Situations are constantly arising in which the literal or strict interpretation of a rule would be contrary to its intent or purpose. (This is the basis of the distinction between the spirit

and the letter of the law.) In such situations the rule ought
not to be applied. Thus, though one can have *some* understanding of a rule without understanding its intent, for an
adequate understanding of the rule one should know the intent behind it. Only so can exceptions to it be made with justice and revisions of it be made with intelligence. (For a perfect understanding of a rule, one should, ideally, understand
how it fits into the system of rules and the system of purposes
they are designed to further.) Now a similar point applies to
moral rules and principles. One can have some understanding of a moral rule without understanding how to apply moral
principles. But for an adequate understanding of a rule one
must know the principles on which it is based—to put it another way, the reasons on which it is established. This is one
reason why reflection on morality is essential to morality.

Let us now consider some examples of moral principles.
What I have called the generalization argument is one. The
generalization principle is another. A third is the principle:
"If the consequences of A's doing x would be undesirable,
then A ought not to do x." Let us call this the *principle of
consequences*. A fourth principle, obviously similar to the
third, is: "It is always wrong to cause unnecessary suffering."
A fifth principle concerns the character of moral rules and
follows from what has already been said about them: "Any
violation of a moral rule must be justified." This principle,
which is an obvious and immediate consequence of the generalization argument, may be called the *principle of justification*.

A little reflection suffices to show that it is impossible for
any of these principles to conflict, though they are all closely
related, and this is a further important difference between
moral rules and principles.

Yet it might be supposed that there is a possibility of a conflict between the generalization argument and the principle
of consequences (and I must say that this is the only case in

which such a supposition seems to me even plausible). For the consequences of an action in a particular case might be undesirable, while the consequences of the general performance of that sort of action might not be undesirable, and this would seem to give us incompatible results. So it is advisable to examine this possibility.

Suppose, then, that if A were to do x the consequences would be undesirable; it should follow, on the principle of consequences, that A ought not to do x. Suppose, also, that if no one were to do x the consequences would be undesirable; it would seem to follow, on the basis of the generalization argument, that everyone, including A, ought to do x. But there are two possibilities here: (1) if everyone were to do x, the consequences would also be undesirable; or (2) if everyone were to do x, the consequences would not be undesirable. In the first case, the generalization argument is what I call "invertible," and nothing follows from it.[8] So in this case the conclusion from the principle of consequences prevails, and A ought not to do x. In the second case, there must be something peculiar about A, or the circumstances in which he is placed, to explain this difference between the consequences of his performing such an action and the consequences of everyone's performing it. If everyone similar to A did x in a similar situation, the consequences would be undesirable, and so in this case, also, A ought not to do x.

I conclude from this that there is no possibility of a conflict between these two principles, and hence that there is no possibility of a conflict between any of them. (Since the appearance of conflict arises out of an insufficiently detailed specification of circumstances, it can always be dispelled.) And this does not have the consequence of creating a class of situations to which they are inapplicable. But there are some important points to be noted about each of the last three

[8] For a discussion of this condition on the application of the generalization argument, see p. 373 of the essay cited above, note 4.

principles I have listed, and it is the intention of the following remarks to bring these out.

1. The principle of consequences states that, if the consequences of A's doing x would be undesirable, then A ought not to do x. (This is, obviously, equivalent to: "If the consequences of A's *not* doing x would be undesirable, then A ought to do x." It is not, however, equivalent to: "If the consequences of A's doing x would be *desirable*, then A ought to do x," and I am not at all sure whether the latter proposition is true.) Now I do not think that anyone has ever questioned or denied this principle, at least explicitly. But there are unquestionably many cases in which it has been violated or disregarded, and it can be misunderstood, especially if the term "undesirable" is not properly understood. This term may be interpreted in either of two senses, with the consequence that there are two ways of interpreting the principle. Though these two ways are consistent with each other, they should be kept distinct.

One sense of "undesirable" is that of "undesirable on the whole." On this interpretation, the principle does not mean that if *some* of the consequences of A's doing x would be undesirable then A ought not to do x. It is perfectly consistent with it for some of the consequences of an act to be desirable and others to be undesirable. And it may well be that, while some of the consequences of an act are undesirable, it is not undesirable, on the whole, for the act to be done. For the desirable consequences may *outweigh* the undesirable ones.

In the second sense of "undesirable" it does not have this proviso of "on the whole." On this interpretation, the fact that some of the consequences of A's doing x would be undesirable is *a* reason for asserting that A ought not to do x, but it is not a conclusive reason. On the basis of this fact one could reasonably presume that it would be wrong for A to do x. This presumption can be rebutted by showing that not all the consequences are undesirable, and that the undesirable consequences are outweighed by (are less important than) the desirable ones; in other words, by showing that the consequences of A's doing x would not be undesirable on the whole. Thus a more adequate, because less elliptical, statement of the principle, on this interpretation, would be: "If the consequences of A's doing x would be undesirable, then A ought not to do x *without a reason or justification*." Statements of the form "A ought to do x," and similar statements, are most usually elliptical in this way.

These brief remarks should make it clear that this principle assumes a good deal less than might at first glance be supposed. It does not by itself determine the meaning of the term "desirable," or what is desirable or undesirable, or how the various consequences of an action are to be weighed against each other in order to determine whether they are undesirable on the whole. Agreement on the principle is quite consistent with disagreement on these latter questions. Indeed, without agreement on the principle, disagreement on these other matters would have no point.

2. A somewhat similar point is relevant to the principle that it is always wrong to cause unnecessary suffering. This principle does not by itself determine whether the suffering caused by an act was or was not necessary or unavoidable. This is determined by other rules, and varies with conditions. But though this principle is somewhat indefinite it does not follow that it is useless. For it sets limits to the rules that are permissible. It is true that, if an act likely to cause suffering can be justified on other grounds, if it is required by some other rule, then the suffering likely to ensue from it would not be regarded as unnecessary. But what this shows is that what this principle requires is that an act likely to cause suffering is one that requires justification, and that the justification must consist in showing that the suffering likely to ensue is unavoidable or not unnecessary.

Thus this principle has a moral rule correlated with it, to

the effect that it is generally wrong to cause others to suffer. Similarly, the rule that stealing is generally wrong has a correlated moral principle, to the effect that stealing for the sake of stealing is always wrong. And correlated with the rule that lying is generally wrong is the principle that lying for the sake of lying (wanton lying) is always wrong, and so on. (There would thus appear to be at least two kinds of moral principles: those that have moral rules correlated with them, and those that do not. But there are of course other differences between moral principles: some refer more directly to actions, some to rules, and some—as in the case of the two most recently mentioned—to the motives or intentions of actions; and some, as should be clear, can be derived from others.)

3. A question may arise about what is meant by a "violation" of a moral rule. It may be said that if someone is justified in doing some act then his act cannot violate any rule, even if it is a member of a class of acts that are generally wrong. But I am using the expression "violation of a rule" in a somewhat wider sense, so that any act of a type that is generally wrong can be said to violate a rule. (Synonymously with this we can speak of an act's conflicting with, or infringing, or breaking a moral rule, or of a discrepancy between an action and a rule.) Thus I shall say that to tell a lie is to violate the rule against lying, to steal something is to violate the rule against stealing, and so on. This is not to be interpreted as entailing that the action is wrong. Also, if there is good reason to believe that someone has stolen something, then there is good reason to believe that his action violates the rule against stealing. In this sort of case the action apparently violates the rule, and such an action is in need of justification. One can, of course, justify himself in this sort of case by showing that he did not *steal* the object, that he had permission to take it, or that it was his in the first place. But there is certainly a difference between showing that one did not really steal, even though he appeared to, and thus did not

really violate a rule, and showing that in the circumstances one was justified in stealing.

The principle of justification states that any action that violates a moral rule is in need of justification. I should say that the converse of this is also true: an action that does not violate a moral rule is not in need of justification. The question whether an act is justified would normally not arise unless there were such a conflict, either real or apparent. For the *demand* that an act be justified implies or presupposes that there is such a conflict, and would be unintelligible if there were not. In other words, to claim that an act *requires* justification is to imply that it is in conflict with some rule—that there is some reason for thinking it to be wrong. If there is no such discrepancy, if there is no reason for thinking the act to be wrong, then the act does not require justification. There are, therefore, cases where the demand that an act be justified may itself require justification.

But, though an action may not require or be in need of justification, it does not follow that it cannot be justified, or that it makes no sense to speak of a justification of it. It seems to me necessary, therefore, to distinguish two senses of "justification," a weak and a strong, or to distinguish those actions (or kinds of actions) that demand justification, because there are reasons for believing them to be wrong, from those that do not demand it, and yet can still be justified or shown to be right. An act can be justified (in the weak sense) though it is not *in need of* justification (in the strong sense). In the former sense of the term, to say that an act is justified is simply to say that it is right, and not to imply that there is some reason for believing it to be wrong. In some uses, to be sure, it seems to imply more than this—it seems to imply that the act has been *shown* to be right. But the distinguishing feature of the two senses is that in the strong sense the term implies that there is some reason for believing the act to be wrong, and thus that it apparently violates a moral rule. This is the sense in which it can be said that an act demands or requires justification. Now the way in which an act that demands justification would be justified differs from the way in which an act that does not would be. One can justify an act of the latter sort merely by showing that there are reasons for it. In justifying an act that demands justification it would not suffice merely to give reasons for it; one would have to show, in addition, that these reasons outweigh the reasons against it.

But it still holds that a justification is not demanded for an action unless there is some question about it. And I am not wedded to the distinction I have just elaborated. Yet if it should be thought unsound, or too artificial, I should hold that it is necessary to recognize two different kinds of demands or requirements, which may be distinguished as those of practice and those of theory. For we can speak of the justification of rules, even where there is no reason against them, and hence no practical demand for it.

III

There are at least three different kinds of moral rules which it is necessary to distinguish. Such rules as the ones against lying, killing, or stealing fall into a special class. These rules are fundamental moral rules. There are also what I propose to call "neutral norms," such as the rules of the road. Third, there are what might be called "local" rules. This class includes various standards, customs, and traditions, peculiar to different groups or communities, as well as such rules as the rule that everyone ought to pay his taxes. All these rules are similar in that a violation of them requires justification. But they are related in somewhat different ways to the generalization argument.

What I have called local rules are less comprehensive, and more closely tied down to their contexts and the purposes that justify them, than fundamental moral rules. Apart from being, as their name implies, more fundamental, the latter do not depend on variations in social or geographical conditions in the way local rules do, owing, perhaps, to their greater comprehensiveness (and generality) and relative freedom from context. It makes no sense to say of the rule to keep promises, for instance, that it may hold for one group of people and not for another. It does make sense to say this of the rule to pay taxes.

But let us consider first what I have called neutral norms. As an example of a neutral norm we may take the rule that everyone is required to drive on the right-hand side of the road. Such rules are *neutral* because it would make no moral difference if their opposites were adopted. This is the important difference between this type of rule and other rules. The rule just mentioned does not apply to people in England, where the rule is to drive on the left (and it might very well have been made a rule to proceed on red and stop on green). There is nothing antecedently (i.e., to the adoption of the rule) wrong about any of these activities. It is wrong (in the United States) to drive on the left-hand side of the road, as a consequence of the fact that the rule has been adopted and people are generally expected to obey it.

I have chosen the term "neutral norm" in analogy to Poincaré's term "neutral hypothesis." The characteristic of a neutral hypothesis is that "the same conclusions would have been reached by taking precisely the opposite," while it is necessary to make some assumption.[9] The characteristic of a neutral norm is that the same results would have been attained by adopting precisely the opposite, while it is necessary to adopt *some* rule.

That it is necessary to have some rule is established by the application of the generalization argument. What would happen if there were no rules for directing and ordering traffic,

[9] Henri Poincaré, "Science and Hypothesis," in *The Foundations of Science* (Lancaster, Pa.: Science Press, 1913), chap. ix, p. 135.

if everyone drove on the same side of the road, or on the side of the road on which he happened to feel like driving? There is no need to specify the details. It is surely clear that this would be, to say the least, extremely inconvenient, and this is sufficient to show that not everyone ought to drive on the same side of the road, and that no one has the right to drive on the side of the road on which he happens, at the moment, to feel like driving. It follows that everyone ought to drive on the right, or on the left—it does not matter which—in accordance with the rule of the community whose roads he is using; unless he has, as he might in special circumstances, good reason for the contrary. It obviously also follows that there must be some rule to prevent catastrophe and serve the needs roads were built to serve. It is clearly indifferent which rule is adopted, so long as it serves this purpose (and is not, on other grounds, obviously unjust or inconvenient).

It should be evident that a neutral norm involves an essential reference to a social need or purpose, which is advanced by the general observance of the rule and would be defeated by the general disregard of it. It is in terms of this need or purpose that it would be disastrous, or undesirable, if there were no such rule, and it is in terms of this need or purpose that the rule must be justified. Of course, a reference to expectations is also involved in the explanation of why it is wrong to disregard such a rule. People generally expect others to obey these rules and normally rely upon their doing so. But it is not wrong to violate such a rule *simply* because people expect and depend upon others to do so. This is no doubt part of the explanation. Yet, if no one obeyed such rules, probably no one would expect anyone to do so. Hence the main reason it would be disastrous if no one obeyed such rules lies in the social needs such nonobservance would frustrate.

Now what I have called local rules also involve an essential reference to social needs and purposes, on which they depend and in terms of which they may be justified.

IV

One instance of a local rule is the rule requiring people to pay taxes. Not every government requires its citizens to pay taxes. The amounts to be paid, and the kinds of taxes to be collected, vary from time to time and from place to place in accordance with different conditions and needs. At a time when there is no need for taxes to be collected, the argument, "What would happen if no one paid taxes?" would be inapplicable. Thus such a rule depends on local conditions in a way in which fundamental moral rules do not. The fundamental moral rules are more like the preconditions for any society or government at all. One cannot avoid the obligation to keep promises or be honest without removing himself from society altogether (and I do not mean in the merely physical sense).

I mentioned before that this class of rules also includes traditions and customs, as well as various standards, of which the standards of fair competition regulating certain business and other activities may be taken as representative. Also in this class are the rules that make up what are known as the "ethical codes" that prevail in different professions.[10] Such rules do not have the comprehensiveness of fundamental moral rules. They apply only to certain groups of people: to those in a certain type of business, or to the members of a certain profession, and, in the case of a custom or tradition, to the members of the society of which it is the custom or tra-

[10] For a useful compilation, see Edgar L. Heermance, *Codes of Ethics* (Burlington, Vt.: Free Press Printing Co., 1924). For an interesting discussion, with further references, see "An Ethical Code for Scientists," by W. Pignan and E. B. Carmichael, *Science*, CXI (1950), 643–47; also *Science*, CXII (1950), 656.

dition. (One who is not a doctor cannot sensibly be accused of "conduct unbecoming a doctor.") They also vary with different conditions. In one community it might be "unfair competition" to open a laundry within three blocks of another laundry; in another community the limit might be five blocks.

Many of these rules are no doubt cruel and unjust, not to say foolish. As with "vestigial relics" in the law, many of them continue to exist and govern conduct long after the need that brought them into existence has ceased to exist, or after the conditions have changed in which they were meant to apply. Nevertheless these rules have a prima facie claim to acceptance. This is shown by what would happen if every one in a community disregarded its customs or traditions. "Imitation of the past," as Justice Holmes has said, *until we have a clear reason for change*, no more needs justification than appetite." [11] To put it another way, these rules are binding simply because they are accepted by a dominant part of the group to which they apply. It may therefore be presumed that the members of the group expect and depend on other members to act in accordance with them. And the value of standards and codes for regulating conduct in need of regulation should not be underestimated. As with neutral

[11] O. W. Holmes, *Collected Legal Papers* (New York: Harcourt, Brace & Co., 1921), p. 290. The phrase "until we have a clear reason for change" is important enough to warrant special emphasis. Compare, on this same general point, the following statement by Whately: "There is a presumption in favour of every *existing* institution. Many of these . . . may be susceptible of alteration for the better; but still the 'burden of proof' lies with him who proposes an alteration; simply, on the ground that since a change is not a good in itself, he who demands a change should show cause for it. No one is *called on* (though he may find it advisable) to defend an existing institution, till some argument is adduced against it; and that argument ought in fairness to prove, not merely an actual inconvenience, but the possibility of a change for the better" (Richard Whately, *Elements of Rhetoric* [7th ed., London: John W. Parker & Son, 1857], Part I, chap. iii, sec. 2, pp. 73–74).

norms, in many cases they actually determine what "ethical" or "unethical" conduct is in a certain situation.

It is no part of my purpose to compile a catalogue of various kinds of local rules. There are of course important differences between standards, traditions, and codes, but it would be an unnecessary digression to take account of them here. What I wish to do here is merely to illustrate the way in which what I have called the generalization argument can generate (demonstrate the need for) and justify such rules. Thus what I propose to do is to present and comment on two actual examples of the application of this principle to establish a local rule.

1. In the first example, the principle is applied, under war conditions, to justify a certain military (or naval) policy.

> It was difficult to get yourself transferred from Alaskan vessels because of seasickness, for if such a policy had prevailed, there would have been no ships there, but it wasn't impossible. . . . Almost everyone on that duty was seasick some of the time, for the small escort vessels patrolled the whole winter long. . . .[12]

This example is almost self-explaining. I might just point out that this application of the principle presupposes that it was necessary, given the need to win the war, for there to be ships in Alaskan waters. If there were no war, or other emergency, there would be no need for such a drastic policy, which would then lose its justification. (To specify the point illustrated by the phrase "but it wasn't impossible" would be to underline the obvious.)

2. In the second example the principle is applied to establish a legal rule.

> "Two systems of water law are in force within the United States —the riparian and the appropriation systems." The system first named prevails in thirty-one of the forty-eight states. Its funda-

[12] Sloan Wilson, "Citation," *New Yorker*, XXVIII, No. 1 (February 23, 1952), 70.

mental principle is "that each riparian proprietor has an equal right to make a reasonable use of the waters of the stream, subject to the equal right of the other riparian proprietors likewise to make a reasonable use." Some of the arid states of the west found this system unsuited to their needs. Division of the water "into small quantities among the various users and on the general principle of equality of right" would be a division "so minute as not to be of advantage to anybody." "It is better in such a region that some have enough and others go without, than that the divison should be so minute as to be of no real economic value." The appropriation system is built upon the recognition of this truth. Its fundamental principle is "that the water user who first puts to beneficial use—irrigation, mining, manufacturing, power, household, or other economic use—the water of a stream, acquires thereby the first right to the water, to the extent reasonably necessary to his use, and that he who is the second to put the water of the stream to beneficial use, acquires the second right, a right similar to the first right, but subordinate thereto, and he who is the third to put it to use acquires the third right, a right subordinate to the other two, and so on throughout the entire series of uses." [13]

It is worth making explicit the exact way in which the generalization argument is involved here. It is through the application of the generalization argument that the difference in the amounts of water available in, say, Arizona and Illinois is determined to be a relevant difference in the circumstances of riparians living in those states; a difference, that is, relevant to the question how rights to the use of the water should be distributed. The fact that one state may have more water than another is not by itself a relevant difference, so long as there is enough to satisfy the needs of all. But, if every riparian in Arizona had the right to use as much water as he needs, there

[13] B. N. Cardozo, *The Growth of the Law* (New Haven: Yale University Press, 1924), pp. 118–19, quoting from Bannister, "Interstate Rights in Interstate Streams in the Arid West," *Harvard Law Review*, XXXVI (1922–23), 960–62. Cardozo comments: "Here we have the conscious departure from a known rule, and the deliberate adoption of a new one, in obedience to the promptings of a social need so obvious and so insistent as to overrun the ancient channel and cut a new one for itself."

would not be enough to go around—none of them would obtain as much as he needs. Hence not every riparian in Arizona ought to have an equal right to the water of that state. On the other hand, since this sort of consequence would not result from allowing every riparian in Illinois to use as much water as he needs, and there is therefore no reason against it, every riparian in Illinois ought to have an equal right to the water of his state. It does not follow, however, that *no* riparian in Arizona should have the right to use as much water as he needs. For the consequences of this, presumably, would be equally undesirable. The fact that, if everyone in Arizona had equal water rights, none would have enough water, sets a problem, which is to determine a fair way of distributing rights to the use of the water. The rule devised, which would be justifiable only under these conditions, is the one set down above.

This last example illustrates particularly well the way in which a local rule is more closely tied to its context, is less comprehensive, than a fundamental moral rule. The rule just mentioned applies only to people in Arizona (and other arid states). Different rules are required by the different conditions in the different states. If Illinois' water supply should sharply decrease, this would be a good reason for changing the rule. Note that these rules are not neutral norms. It is not indifferent which rule is adopted.

V

Let us turn to the question of justifying fundamental moral rules. The procedure, as already indicated, is the same in every case. Moral rules are established by means of the generalization argument. A rule that cannot be derived from an application of the generalization argument cannot be justified.

Since the procedure in every case is the same, it does not matter which rule we select to exemplify it. Let us take the rule that lying is wrong. What is the proof of this? Since to justify a moral rule is equivalent to explaining why a certain kind of action is generally right or wrong, to justify the rule against lying is equivalent to explaining why lying is wrong. Thus it will be sufficient to answer the question, "Why is it wrong to lie?"

I cannot refrain from pointing out how utterly fantastic it would be to answer the question, "Why is it wrong to lie?" (or any question of this kind) by saying, "Lying is wrong because I disapprove of it," or, "Lying is wrong because most people disapprove of it." This would not be an answer at all. Lying is not wrong *because* it is disapproved, that is, *regarded as wrong*. It would be more plausible to say that lying is regarded as wrong because it is wrong, for to explain why lying is wrong is to justify regarding it as wrong. But the fact that lying is disapproved is as irrelevant to explaining why it is wrong as is the fact that one who lies is likely to be punished for it. It is no answer to say, "Lying is wrong because I'll hit you if you lie." This goes no way to show that, or why, lying is *wrong*. If someone should ask for a reason why he ought not to lie, the assertion that he will be hit or otherwise punished if he does might be a relevant consideration. The fact that someone will be punished if he does something may be a good prudential reason for not doing it. If what he can gain from the lying will not compensate for the punishment, then he would be well advised not to lie. But this has no tendency to show that lying is morally wrong, that he has the duty not to lie. The child will be hurt if he touches the fire, and this is a good reason why he should not touch the fire. But this has no tendency to show that it would be morally wrong to do so. Similar considerations apply to the answer in terms of what is disapproved. This might serve as a device to keep someone from lying. We often have to use such devices. But it is irrelevant to the question why it is wrong to lie. For an act that is right might be punished or disapproved. And it is wrong to lie even in those situations in which one can get away with it without being disapproved or punished. The perfect crime is one that goes undetected or unpunished. It is not one that is justified.

Of course, in some instances the fact that an act is generally disapproved can create a presumption against it. But this fact, by itself, could not *make* it wrong, or constitute its wrongness. For this presumption, like others, can be rebutted, and to rebut it would be to show that the act is not wrong even though it is widely and strongly disapproved. The existence of a widespread disapproval of some practice is a major source of moral problems and can be no automatic answer to them. The fact of social disapproval, furthermore, as the source (and sometimes the consequence) of customs and traditions, can establish only local rules, not fundamental ones.

The reason lying is wrong should be obvious from what has already been said. Lying is wrong because of what would happen if everyone lied. It would be nothing short of disastrous if everyone were to lie whenever he wished to, if lying became the rule and truth-telling the exception (which is, social cynics to the contrary, not the prevailing practice, but the opposite of it).[14] Hence it follows that lying is generally wrong, or that no one has the right to lie without a reason, and that the mere wish or desire to lie is never a sufficient justification.

This last point, that the mere wish or desire to lie is never a sufficient justification, is shown by the further application

[14] The fundamental character of such rules is brought out quite vividly by Mill in the following passage: "The moral rules which forbid mankind to hurt one another (in which we must never forget to include wrongful interference with each other's freedom) are more vital to human well-being than any maxims, however important, which only point out the best mode of managing some department of human affairs. . . . It is their observance which alone preserves peace among human beings: if obedience to them were not the rule, and disobedience the exception, everyone would see in everyone else an enemy, against whom he must be perpetually guarding himself" (*Utilitarianism*, chap. v, p. 55).

of the generalization principle. For suppose that it were, and that I claimed the right to lie on the ground that I wanted to. Then every similar person, and that is, in this context, everyone who wants to lie, would thereby have the right to lie; that is to say, everyone would have the right to lie whenever he wanted to. The consequences of everyone's doing this, as I have already pointed out, would be nothing short of disastrous, and hence not everyone could have this right. But to "reason" or try to justify oneself in this way really involves a contradiction, for it is to claim to be an exception to a rule on grounds that would make everyone an exception. If everyone had the right to lie whenever he wanted to, then everyone would have the right to do whatever he pleased under any circumstances whatsoever, and this also, I should say, is self-contradictory.

I have said that the rule against lying is a typical case, and that all moral rules are established by the undesirable, even disastrous, consequences that would follow if everyone were generally to act contrary to them. It follows from this that moral rules are not isolated or independent of each other; they are connected through the fact that they are established through the application of the generalization argument. But it does not follow that the consequences of the general violation of one rule may not differ in an important way from the consequences of the general violation of another rule. It can be argued, for instance, that it would be impossible for lying to become the rule and truth-telling the exception, for on this supposition there could be no use of language, and thus no possibility of lying. If everyone were to lie, either regularly or promiscuously, so that it would be impossible to tell when anyone was speaking honestly, eventually no one could speak. We could not generally presume, as we do, that people's assertions are made honestly. The use of language is based on the assumption that, even though people are very often mistaken in what they say, and often use words to deceive, it is not so always or for the most part. For no one could learn a language if his teachers were generally to lie to him; there would be no regularity in the use or reference of the words he was "taught." In the case of other rules, corresponding though somewhat different things can be said.

VI

It should be clear that the generalization argument does not establish moral rules as holding always or in all circumstances. This is a consequence of the generalization principle: If not everyone has the right to act in a certain way, then no one has the right to act in that way without a reason. Hence, if it would be undesirable for everyone to lie, no one has the right to lie without a reason. This obviously implies that it is possible for the rule to have exceptions. Whether a particular case is an exception to the rule is determined by specifying in a more detailed way the circumstances of the act in question. If the circumstances of the act are such that in those, or similar, circumstances it would not be undesirable for everyone to act in that way, then in those circumstances the act would not be wrong. (But this requires further qualifications that cannot be elaborated here. What is important is the principle on which the circumstances are specified.) That moral rules can have exceptions, and thus do not hold always, is, as already mentioned, also required by the fact that they can, in particular instances, come into conflict. But, if moral rules are derivable from the generalization argument, as I have been maintaining, then to maintain of any moral rule that it holds without exception would be self-contradictory. It would, for instance, be self-contradictory to maintain that lying is always, and not just generally, wrong, because the reasons that establish the rule are the very same reasons that, in certain circumstances, would suffice to override it. And I should say that one who maintains that lying is always wrong, without giving any reasons in support of the assertion, is merely saying or indicating something about his attitudes or feelings or the way he would react to a lie.

It follows from what has been said that in cases in which rules conflict, in which there are conflicting claims or obligations, the generalization argument provides the criterion for deciding or mediating between them. For the action will be right in the particular circumstances only if it would be right for everyone in similar circumstances. Thus, to show of a certain act in these circumstances that it is not wrong, one must show that the consequences of everyone's acting in that way in similar circumstances would not be undesirable. It can be shown that it is a duty, and hence wrong not to act in that way, if the consequences of no one's acting in that way in similar circumstances would be undesirable. (The notorious vagueness of moral rules, resulting from the vagueness of such terms as "lying" and "stealing," can, I should say, be eliminated or cut down by the same process through which the rules are established. For in the question, "What would happen if everyone lied?" one can substitute any proposed definition or analysis of "lying.")

But what I am claiming about the generalization argument in relation to moral rules can perhaps be made clearer by some explicit indication of what I am not claiming.

I am not claiming, in the first place, that in the sort of situation just mentioned, in which there are conflicting claims or obligations, or in the justification of an action generally, the generalization argument is in fact, or must be, always invoked or explicitly appealed to. It is not always or even regularly. Nor need it be. Nevertheless it is appealed to implicitly or tacitly. From the fact that a principle is not mentioned it does not follow that it is not used or presupposed. And the generalization argument, I am maintaining, is presupposed in every case in which an attempt is made to justify or give reasons for an action. It should really be obvious that in giving a justification it is not necessary to make an explicit appeal to the generalization argument. The generalization argument is in practice rarely appealed to except in cases in which rules conflict, in which there are conflicting considerations, or in which there seems to be no ordinary moral rule that is applicable. For it is very often sufficient merely to invoke a rule or to point out the existence of a right. Thus, if someone wants to know why it would be wrong for him to act in a certain way, it is often sufficient to point out that it would be a case of stealing (or lying, or taking advantage of someone else, etc.), and that stealing (or lying, etc.) is wrong. Yet, even though the generalization argument is not explicitly mentioned here, it is necessarily involved. For it is involved in the explanation of why stealing is wrong. And the argument just presented obviously presupposes that what is wrong in one case is wrong in all.

I am not claiming, furthermore, that the generalization argument must be explicitly invoked in explaining why a certain *kind* of action is wrong. In many cases it suffices to point out the sort of consequences actions of the kind in question may reasonably be expected to have. Such acts as lying, stealing, being cruel to others, generally have mischievous consequences in the particular case. Someone may reasonably be expected to suffer as a consequence of such an action. There would thus appear to be a significant difference between acts of this kind and acts like refusing to pay taxes or avoiding military service or, generally, failing to do one's part in a common enterprise the success of which depends on the cooperation of everyone (or nearly everyone) concerned. For the mischievous effects of dishonesty are much more evident than the mischievous effects of the failure to vote or pay taxes of just one person, or a few persons. (And lying is wrong in itself; not voting is not.[15] To tell a lie one must *intend* to deceive.)

[15] If the expression "wrong in itself" can be used by a utilitarian, no one should find it peculiar. Mill used the expression in the opening

It is in fact to actions of the latter kind that the generalization argument seems to be most often explicitly applied in
practice. The reason why lying is wrong seems more readily
apparent than the reason why it is wrong not to pay one's
taxes. The direct consequences of failing to pay one's taxes
are obscure or seem trifling. Nevertheless, if someone does
not see why lying is wrong, or why it is wrong for *him* to lie
(for it may be lots of fun, and is often very useful), then it
is necessary to make an explicit appeal to the generalization argument. It is wrong to lie because of what would happen if everyone lied. And it is wrong for *him* to lie because
it is wrong for others to lie to him. "How would you like it
if everyone were to lie to you, or take away your property,
or go out of his way to make your life miserable?" Though
one can very well like to lie to others while not liking others
to lie to him, no one can sensibly claim that it would be
wrong for others to lie to him yet not wrong for him to lie
to them. In such a statement "wrong" could mean no more
than "I wouldn't like it."

These considerations indicate that there is a difference between the types of actions involved in fundamental moral
rules and those involved in other kinds of moral rules (or at
least some other kinds). In the case of lying, or stealing, or
cruelty, there is a definitely assignable individual or group of
individuals whose rights or interests would be violated. In the
case of attempting to avoid one's obligations to one's government there is no assignable individual or group whose rights
would be violated. And few of us feel in ourselves the power
to make the government suffer. Thus the mischievous consequences of this sort of act are not so vividly apparent. One
must appeal to *principle*, and not merely to facts. "To do this

sentence of *The Subjection of Women* (1869): ". . . the principle
which regulates the existing social relations between the two sexes—the
legal subordination of one sex to the other—is wrong in itself, and now
one of the chief hindrances to human improvement. . . ."

is to take advantage of others." Furthermore the act is not reciprocating: the government cannot do the same to us (though it can make us suffer in other ways).

It would be a mistake, however, to suppose from this that fundamental rules are to be distinguished from others on the ground that the latter are governed only by the generalization argument, whereas the former are governed solely by the principle of consequences. It is true, as I have just been maintaining, that the generalization argument has a more immediate or apparent application to rules that, described generally, require one to play his part in a common enterprise the success of which depends on everyone concerned doing his part. It is true also that fundamental rules are governed by the principle of consequences, so that the generalization argument is not the only principle relevant to them. Yet the principle of consequences is itself involved in the generalization argument (which is really a generalization from it).[16] Furthermore, where the consequences of the violation of a moral rule in a particular case would not be undesirable, the principle of consequences would not apply, whereas the generalization argument very well might. If the circumstances of the case are such that the consequences of everyone's acting in that way in those circumstances would be undesirable, then the act is wrong, and it is irrelevant that the consequences of one person's acting in that way in those circumstances would

[16] It may be useful to explain what I mean when I say that the generalization argument is a generalization from the principle of consequences. The principle of consequences (C) states: If the consequences of A's doing x would be undesirable, then A does not have the right to do x. The following principle (GC) is a simple generalization of C: If the consequences of everyone's doing x would be undesirable, then not everyone has the right to do x. Now the generalization principle (GP) may be stated as follows: If not everyone has the right to do x, then not anyone (no one) has the right to do x. The generalization argument (if the consequences of everyone's doing x would be undesirable, then no one has the right to do x) clearly follows from GP and GC.

not be undesirable. And, though this sort of case is not governed by the principle of consequences, it is governed by the rules themselves. For one is not justified in violating a moral rule simply because the consequences of his particular violation would not be undesirable. (It is not even sufficient for the consequences to be positively desirable.)

Finally, I am not claiming, nor do I wish to imply, that the application of the generalization argument to the situations I have mentioned is an easy or automatic process. In many cases it is a matter of the utmost difficulty. For, apart from the difficulty of distinguishing relevant from irrelevant features, there is the difficulty of determining what the consequences are likely to be, and there is the further difficulty of evaluating these consequences. And about these various difficulties I have said, if not absolutely nothing, certainly very little.

VII

I have been arguing that moral principles are to be distinguished from moral rules by the fact that the former hold in all circumstances and do not admit of exceptions; that principles are invariant and do not vary with changes in circumstances or conditions; and that it is impossible for moral principles to conflict with one another. I have, furthermore, tried to show how moral principles—especially the two that I have called the generalization principle and the generalization argument—are involved in the establishment of moral rules, and how, in particular, they can establish different rules in different circumstances. In this connection, I distinguished between fundamental rules, local rules, and neutral norms. Local rules, I maintained, depend on local conditions in a way that fundamental rules do not, and hence are peculiar to, and differ with, different groups and communities—that is to say, different circumstances. Neutral norms are local rules that are conventional in a way that other rules are not, but both neutral norms and local rules depend on social needs or purposes that are advanced by their general observance and would be frustrated or defeated by their general violation. Hence changes in these needs or purposes would require changes in these rules.

I mention all this now not just to summarize the main features of an already complex argument, but to bring out the relevance of what I have been saying to the idea of cultural or moral relativity, and the closely associated theory of ethical relativism. By cultural relativity (or diversity) I understand the empirically ascertained fact that there are a great many different and even conflicting rules and practices prevailing at different times and in different places, so that (what at least appears to be) the same act may be regarded as right in one place and wrong in another. By ethical relativism I understand the theory that moral ideas are necessarily "relative to" a particular society, in the sense that they reflect the "standpoint" of some particular society and only "hold for" that society, so that in case of a conflict between these different standards there is no way of impartially or objectively deciding between them. Thus on this theory all moral judgments are incomplete unless they specify "the standpoint" from which they are made, and it is a further consequence of it that moral judgments are really expressions of the attitude or characteristic bias of a particular group. On this view, in other words, there is nothing that can correctly be said to *be* right or wrong; it is only a question of what is *called* "right" or "wrong," and by what group it is so called.

The fact of moral diversity, the fact that there are varieties of moralities and moral codes, is of course a main source of the theory of ethical relativism. But it is not sufficient, by itself, to give rise to this theory. For this purpose other assumptions are required.

This theory arises, in the first place, from a failure to distinguish the invariant moral principles from the variable conditions that, in accordance with these principles, require or permit a variety of different rules and practices. Though practices and rules may be "relative," it does not follow that principles are. Yet this theory supposes that it does. It should really be obvious that moral principles, and I have in mind here especially the generalization principle and the generalization argument, do not require any uniformity of practices in different cultures. For they do not require any uniformity of practices in different circumstances. What is right in one context or set of circumstances may not be right in another, and differences in social or geographical conditions can count as relevant differences in circumstances. Thus what is right in Pomerania need not be right in Polynesia, or among the Dobuans, or in Rome. What is puzzling is that it should ever have been supposed that it should be so. For this general point, that moral principles are consistent with and allow for a wide variety of rules and practices, has often been made before (and from a variety of "standpoints"). It was made, for instance, in 1758, by Richard Price:

> Though all men, in all cases, judged rightly what is virtue and right behaviour, there would still prevail a very considerable variety in their moral practices in different ages and countries. The reason is obvious: In different ages and circumstances of the world, the same practices often have not the same connexions, tendencies, and effects. . . . New obligations must arise, and the proprieties of conduct must vary, as new connexions take place, and new customs, laws, and political constitutions are introduced. Many practices, very warrantable and proper under one form of government, or in the first establishment of a community, or amongst people of a particular genius, and where particular regulations and opinions prevail, may be quite wrong in another state of things, or amongst people of other characters and customs.[17]

[17] Richard Price, *Review of the Principal Questions in Morals*, ed. D. Daiches Raphael (Oxford: Clarendon Press, 1948), chap. vii, p. 175. See also, for this same general point, W. D. Ross, *Foundations of Ethics* (Oxford: Clarendon Press, 1939), pp. 18–19; F. C. Sharp, *Ethics* (New York: Century Co., 1928), chap. xi; M. R. Cohe··

This point should be fairly clear with respect to local rules, since I have already pointed out that such rules vary with and depend on conditions and needs that are different at different times and places, and this is in fact the defining feature of such rules. With respect to fundamental rules, however, it may not be so obvious. For there are societies in which such rules as the rule against lying are not recognized at all, in which it is not thought wrong to lie, or at least in which the scope of the rule is drastically restricted, so that there are very few persons to whom it is thought wrong to lie.[18] But the fact that in some societies it is not wrong, or is not thought wrong, to lie, is not inconsistent with the rule that lying is generally wrong. For the rule does not say that it is always wrong to lie; and under certain sets of conditions, which may prevail in certain societies, the presumption of the rule may be *inoperative*. Where there is a recognized and well-defined class of exceptions to a rule, it is possible to formulate a subsidiary rule stating the conditions under which the fundamental rule does not apply, in which its presumption is inoperative. If the circumstances governed by the subsidiary rule should be-

---

Reason and Nature (New York: Harcourt, Brace & Co., 1931), pp. 349, 411–12; and Morris Ginsberg, *Reason and Unreason in Society* (London: Longman's Green & Co., 1947), pp. 305–7.

[18] This sort of case is discussed by A. Macbeath, *Experiments in Living* (London: Macmillan & Co., 1952), pp. 370–75, who says: "If a man believes, as the Bantu does, that any of his neighbours may be, and that some of them in fact are, endowed with supernatural powers which may be used to do him or his neighbours harm; and if he further believes that giving them information provides them with the means of using these powers, we have a state of affairs in which not mutual trust and confidence but mutual suspicion and fear are likely to flourish. In such circumstances, truth-telling is not likely to be regarded as a virtue except in situations like giving evidence in court, where truth-telling is likely to result in good to others and lying in harm to them" (pp. 372–73). Of course, in these matters it is essential to distinguish between explanation and justification. In all such cases where a certain practice is explained by a certain peculiar belief, there is always the question whether the belief is justified.

come general, so that they are no longer exceptional, the subsidiary rule may take precedence. So there may be whole societies, or whole periods of time, where people are governed more by the subsidiary rule than by the fundamental rule. Such a set of conditions would be the "state of nature" so vividly described by Hobbes. Where conditions of mutual suspicion and hostility prevail, so that telling the truth is, in general, likely to place one in a position of considerable disadvantage, there is, in general, no obligation to tell the truth. In such circumstances lying is (or is thought to be) a means of survival, and in such circumstances the consequences of the general violation of the rule would not be undesirable. (What is undesirable, presumably, is the existence of such a situation, but this is something else again; and of course people in such circumstances could not lie all the time, or to everyone.) Now in certain societies and in certain areas, existing even today, people are as close to living in a state of nature (in which the life of man is "solitary, poor, nasty, brutish, and short") as it is possible to come. (Compare conditions in a concentration camp, or in a den of thieves, or "on the waterfront.")

But, in the second place, this theory also arises out of the peculiar and question-begging assumption that if a certain practice prevails in a certain place then it is necessarily right in that place, that if a rule is not *recognized* by the members of a certain group then it does not *apply* to the members of that group. This assumption is not just peculiar; it is self-contradictory. One could, on this assumption, organize a group of thieves, who, by the mere fact that they like to steal, would be justified in stealing. On this view, one could justify himself in doing anything whatsoever merely by refusing to recognize any rule against it or by inculcating a taste for it. (For one person can constitute himself a society.) I have already pointed out how this is self-contradictory. If I were suddenly to hit you on the head with the jagged end of a broken bottle, for no reason at all, or "just because I felt like it," this would be immoral, and there is no possibility of justifying such an action (as distinct from getting away with it). For this is a case of wanton assault, of cruelty for the sake of cruelty, and this is always wrong, irrespective of circumstances. After the Indians in the Hudson Bay territory had obtained guns, it is reported, they "used to hunt Eskimos for sport, as we hunt bear or deer. . . . When eventually the Eskimos got guns, the Indians left them alone." [19] No doubt hunting Eskimos for sport was, at least for a time, part of the accepted practice of this Indian community. But by no stretch of the imagination does it follow that it was therefore justified, and I have already set forth the principles on which this can be shown. It is one thing to record a practice; it is another to determine its moral standing.

This is, to be sure, a topic of the greatest complexity, and I do not pretend to have said all there is to be said about it. I have mentioned this matter here not solely because of the obvious relevance to it of the argument I have been presenting, but also because it raises problems of the greatest importance. For the observation of different and apparently conflicting codes and practices is a major source of *moral* problems, not just of problems of ethical theory or moral philosophy. Moral problems are not simply problems of what to do; they are also problems of what to believe. With respect to morality, at any rate, there can be no fixed and precise line between theory and practice.

[19] *New Yorker*, XXV, No. 17 (June 18, 1949), 30.

J. O. URMSON

Saints and Heroes

Moral philosophers tend to discriminate, explicitly or implicitly, three types of action from the point of view of moral worth. First, they recognize actions that are a duty, or obligatory, or that we ought to perform, treating these terms as approximately synonymous; second, they recognize actions that are right in so far as they are permissible from a moral standpoint and not ruled out by moral considerations, but that are not morally required of us, like the lead of this or that card at bridge; third, they recognize actions that are wrong, that we ought not to do. Some moral philosophers, indeed, could hardly discriminate even these three types of action consistently with the rest of their philosophy; Moore, for example, could hardly recognize a class of morally indifferent actions, permissible but not enjoined, since it is to be presumed that good or ill of some sort will result from the most trivial of our actions. But most moral philosophers recognize these three types of action and attempt to provide a moral theory that will make intelligible such a threefold classification.

To my mind this threefold classification, or any classification that is merely a variation on or elaboration of it, is totally inadequate to the facts of morality; any moral theory that leaves room only for such a classification will in consequence also be inadequate. My main task in this paper will be to show the inadequacy of such a classification by drawing attention to two of the types of action that most conspicuously lie outside such a classification; I shall go on to hazard some views on what sort of theory will most easily cope with the facts to which I draw attention, but the facts are here the primary interest.

We sometimes call a person a saint, or an action saintly, using the word "saintly" in a purely moral sense with no religious implications; also we sometimes call a person a hero or an action heroic. It is too clear to need argument that the words "saint" and "hero" are at least normally used in such a way as to be favorably evaluative; it would be impossible to claim that this evaluation is always moral, for clearly we sometimes call a person a saint when evaluating him religiously rather than morally and may call a person the hero of a game or athletic contest in which no moral qualities were displayed, but I shall take it that no formal argument is necessary to show that at least sometimes we use both words for moral evaluation.

If "hero" and "saint" can be words of moral evaluation, we may proceed to the attempt to make explicit the criteria that we implicitly employ for their use in moral contexts. It appears that we so use them in more than one type of situation, and that there is a close parallel between the ways in which the two terms "hero" and "saint" are used; we shall here notice three types of situation in which they are used which seem to be sufficiently different to merit distinction. As the first two types of situation to be noticed are ones that can be readily subsumed under the threefold classification mentioned above, it will be sufficient here to note them and pass on to the third type of situation, which, since it cannot be subsumed under that classification, is for the purposes of this paper the most interesting.

A person may be called a saint (1) if he does his duty regularly in contexts in which inclination, desire, or self-interest would lead most people not to do it, and does so as a result of exercising abnormal self-control; parallel to this a person may be called a hero (1) if he does his duty in contexts in which terror, fear, or a drive to self-preservation would lead most men not to do it, and does so by exercising abnormal self-control. Similarly for actions: an action may be called saintly (1) if it is a case of duty done by virtue of self-control in a context in which most men would be led astray by inclination or self-interest, and an action may be called heroic (1) if it is a case of duty done by virtue of self-control in a context in which most men would be led astray by fear or a drive for self-preservation. The only difference between the saintly and the heroic in this sort of situation is that the one involves resistance to desire and self-interest; the other, resistance to fear and self-preservation. This is quite a clear difference, though there may be marginal cases, or cases in which motives were mixed, in which it would be equally appropriate to call an action indifferently saintly or heroic. It is easy to give examples of both the heroic and the saintly as distinguished above: the unmarried daughter does the saintly deed of staying at home to tend her ailing and widowed father; the terrified doctor heroically stays by his patients in a plague-ridden city.

A person may be called a saint (2) if he does his duty in contexts in which inclination or self-interest would lead most men not to do it, not, as in the previous paragraph, by abnormal self-control, but without effort; parallel to this a person may be called a hero (2) if he does his duty in contexts in which fear would lead most men not to do it, and does so without effort. The corresponding accounts of a saintly (2) or heroic (2) action can easily be derived. Here we have the

conspicuously virtuous deed, in the Aristotelian sense, as op-
posed to the conspicuously self-controlled, encratic deed of
the previous paragraph. People thus purged of temptation or
disciplined against fear may be rare, but Aristotle thought
there could be such; there is a tendency today to think of such
people as merely lucky or unimaginative, but Aristotle thought
more highly of them than of people who need to exercise self-
control.

It is clear that, in the two types of situation so far considered, we are dealing with actions that fall under the concept of duty. Roughly, we are calling a person saintly or heroic
because he does his duty in such difficult contexts that most
men would fail in them. Since for the purposes of this paper
I am merely conceding that we do use the term "saintly" and
"heroic" in these ways, it is unnecessary here to spend time
arguing that we do so use them or in illustrating such uses. So
used, the threefold classification of 'actions whose adequacy
I wish to deny can clearly embrace them. I shall therefore
pass immediately to a third use of the terms "heroic" and
"saintly" which I am not merely willing to concede but
obliged to establish.

I contend, then, that we may also call a person a saint
(3) if he does actions that are far beyond the limits of his
duty, whether by control of contrary inclination and interest
or without effort; parallel to this we may call a person a hero
(3) if he does actions that are far beyond the bounds of his
duty, whether by control of natural fear or without effort.
Such actions are saintly (3) or heroic (3). Here, as it seems
to me, we have the hero or saint, heroic or saintly deed, par
excellence; until now we have been considering but minor
saints and heroes. We have considered the, certainly, heroic
action of the doctor who does his duty by sticking to his
patients in a plague-stricken city; we have now to consider
the case of the doctor who, no differently situated from count-
less other doctors in other places, volunteers to join the de-

pleted medical forces in that city. Previously we were considering the soldier who heroically does his duty in the face of
such dangers as would cause most to shirk—the sort of man
who is rightly awarded the Military Medal in the British
Army; we have now to consider the case of the soldier who
does more than his superior officers would ever ask him to
do—the man to whom, often posthumously, the Victoria
Cross is awarded. Similarly, we have to turn from saintly self-
discipline in the way of duty to the dedicated, self-effacing
life in the service of others which is not even contemplated
by the majority of upright, kind, and honest men, let alone
expected of them.

Let us be clear that we are not now considering cases of
natural affection, such as the sacrifice made by a mother for
her child; such cases may be said with some justice not to fall
under the concept of morality but to be admirable in some
different way. Such cases as are here under consideration may
be taken to be as little bound up with such emotions as affection as any moral action may be. We may consider an example of what is meant by "heroism" (3) in more detail to bring
this out.

We may imagine a squad of soldiers to be practicing the
throwing of live hand grenades; a grenade slips from the hand
of one of them and rolls on the ground near the squad; one of
them sacrifices his life by throwing himself on the grenade
and protecting his comrades with his own body. It is quite
unreasonable to suppose that such a man must be impelled
by the sort of emotion that he might be impelled by if his
best friend were in the squad; he might only just have joined
the squad; it is clearly an action having moral status. But if
the soldier had not thrown himself on the grenade would he
have failed in his duty? Though clearly he is superior in some
way to his comrades, can we possibly say that they failed in
their duty by not trying to be the one who sacrificed himself?
If he had not done so, could anyone have said to him, "You

ought to have thrown yourself on that grenade"? Could a
superior have decently ordered him to do it? The answer to
all these questions is plainly negative. We clearly have here
a case of a moral action, a heroic action, which cannot be
subsumed under the classification whose inadequacy we are
exposing.

But someone may not be happy with this conclusion, and
for more respectable reasons than a desire to save the traditional doctrine. He may reason as follows: in so far as that
soldier had time to feel or think at all, he presumably felt
that he ought to do that deed; he considered it the proper
thing to do; he, if no one else, might have reproached himself
for failing to do his duty if he had shirked the deed. So, it
may be argued, if an act presents itself to us in the way this
act may be supposed to have presented itself to this soldier,
then it is our duty to do it; we have no option. This objection
to my thesis clearly has some substance, but it involves a misconception of what is at issue. I have no desire to present the
act of heroism as one that is naturally regarded as optional
by the hero, as something he might or might not do; I concede
that he might regard himself as being obliged to act as he
does. But if he were to survive the action only a modesty so
excessive as to appear false could make him say, "I only did
my duty," for we know, and he knows, that he has done more
than duty requires. Further, though he might say to himself
that so to act was a duty, he could not say so even beforehand
to anyone else, and no one else could ever say it. Subjectively,
we may say, at the time of action, the deed presented itself
as a duty, but it was not a duty.

Another illustration, this time of saintliness, may help. It is
recorded by Bonaventura that after Francis of Assisi had
finished preaching to the birds on a celebrated occasion his
companions gathered around him to praise and admire. But
Francis himself was not a bit pleased; he was full of self-
reproach that he had hitherto failed in what he now consid-

ered to be his duty to preach to the feathered world. There is indeed no degree of saintliness that a suitable person may not come to consider it to be his duty to achieve. Yet there is a world of difference between this failure to have preached hitherto to the birds and a case of straightforward breach of duty, however venial. First, Francis could without absurdity reproach himself for his failure to do his duty, but it would be quite ridiculous for anyone else to do so, as one could have done if he had failed to keep his vows, for example. Second, it is not recorded that Francis ever reproached anyone else for failure to preach to the birds as a breach of duty. He could claim this action for himself as a duty and could perhaps have exhorted others to preach to the birds; but there could be no question of reproaches for not so acting.

To sum up on this point, then, it seems clear that there is no action, however quixotic, heroic, or saintly, which the agent may not regard himself as obliged to perform, as much as he may feel himself obliged to tell the truth and to keep his promises. Such actions do not present themselves as optional to the agent when he is deliberating; but, since he alone can call such an action of his a duty, and then only from the deliberative viewpoint, only for himself and not for others, and not even for himself as a piece of objective reporting, and since nobody else can call on him to perform such an act as they can call on him to tell the truth and to keep his promises, there is here a most important difference from the rock-bottom duties which are duties for all and from every point of view, and to which anyone may draw attention. Thus we need not deny the points made by our imaginary objector in order to substantiate the point that some acts of heroism and saintliness cannot be adequately subsumed under the concept of duty.

Let us then take it as established that we have to deal in ethics not with a simple trichotomy of duties, permissible actions, and wrong actions, or any substantially similar conceptual scheme, but with something more complicated. We have to add at least the complication of actions that are certainly of moral worth but that fall outside the notion of a duty and seem to go beyond it, actions worthy of being called heroic or saintly. It should indeed be noted that heroic and saintly actions are not the sole, but merely conspicuous, cases of actions that exceed the basic demands of duty; there can be cases of disinterested kindness and generosity, for example, that are clearly more than basic duty requires and yet hardly ask for the high titles, "saintly" and "heroic." Indeed, every case of "going the second mile" is a case in point, for it cannot be one's duty to go the second mile in the same basic sense as it is to go the first—otherwise it could be argued first that it is one's duty to go two miles and therefore that the spirit of the rule of the second mile requires that one go altogether four miles, and by repetition one could establish the need to go every time on an infinite journey. It is possible to go just beyond one's duty by being a little more generous, forbearing, helpful, or forgiving than fair dealing demands, or to go a very long way beyond the basic code of duties with the saint or the hero. When I here draw attention to the heroic and saintly deed, I do so merely in order to have conspicuous cases of a whole realm of actions that lie outside the trichotomy I have criticized and therefore, as I believe, outside the purview of most ethical theories.

Before considering the implications for ethics of the facts we have up to now been concerned to note, it might be of value to draw attention to a less exalted parallel to these facts. If we belong to a club there will be rules of the club, written or unwritten, calling upon us to fulfill certain basic requirements that are a condition of membership, and that may be said to be the duties of membership. It may perhaps be such a basic requirement that we pay a subscription. It will probably be indifferent whether we pay this subscription by check or in cash—both procedures will be "right"—and almost certainly it will be quite indifferent what sort of hat we wear at the meetings. Here, then, we have conformity to rule which is the analogue of doing one's duty, breach of rule which is the analogue of wrongdoing, and a host of indifferent actions, in accordance with the traditional trichotomy. But among the rule-abiding members of such a club what differences there can be! It is very likely that there will be one, or perhaps two or three, to whose devotion and loyal service the success of the club is due far more than to the activities of all the other members together; these are the saints and the heroes of the clubs, who do more for them by far than any member could possibly be asked to do, whose many services could not possibly be demanded in the rules. Behind them come a motley selection, varying from the keen to the lukewarm, whose contributions vary in value and descend sometimes to almost nothing beyond what the rules demand. The moral contribution of people to society can vary in value in the same way.

So much, then, for the simple facts to which I have wished to draw attention. They are simple facts and, unless I have misrepresented them, they are facts of which we are all, in a way, perfectly well aware. It would be absurd to suggest that moral philosophers have hitherto been unaware of the existence of saints and heroes and have never even alluded to them in their works. But it does seem that these facts have been neglected in their general, systematic accounts of morality. It is indeed easy to see that on some of the best-known theories there is no room for such facts. If for Moore, and for most utilitarians, any action is a duty that will produce the greatest possible good in the circumstances, for them the most heroic self-sacrifice or saintly self-forgetfulness will be duties on all fours with truth-telling and promise-keeping. For Kant, beyond the counsels of prudence and the rules of skill, there is only the categorical imperative of duty, and every duty is equally and utterly binding on all men; it is true that he recognizes the limiting case of the holy will, but the holy will is not a will that goes beyond duty but a will that is beyond morality through being incapable of acting except in accordance with the imperative. The nearest to an equivalent to a holy will in the cases we have been noting is the saintly will in the second sense we distinguished—the will that effortlessly does its duty when most would fail—but this is not a true parallel and in any case does not fall within the class of moral actions that go beyond duty to which our attention is primarily given. It is also true that Kant recognized virtues and talents as having conditional value, but not moral value, whereas the acts of heroism and saintliness we have considered have full moral worth, and their value is as unconditional as anyone could wish. Without committing ourselves to a scholarly examination of Kant's ethical works, it is surely evident that Kant could not consistently do justice to the facts before us. Intuitionism seems to me so obscurantist that I should not wish to prophesy what an intuitionist might feel himself entitled to say; but those intuitionists with whose works I am acquainted found their theories on an intuition of the fitting, the prima facie duty or the claim; the act that has this character to the highest degree at any time is a duty. While they recognize greater and lesser, stronger and weaker, claims, this is only in order to be able to deal with the problem of the conflict of duties; they assign no place to the act that, while not a duty, is of high moral importance.

Simple utilitarianism, Kantianism, and intuitionism, then, have no obvious theoretical niche for the saint and the hero. It is possible, no doubt, to revise these theories to accommodate the facts, but until so modified successfully they must surely be treated as unacceptable, and the modifications required might well detract from their plausibility. The intuitionists, for example, might lay claim to the intuition of a nonnatural characteristic of saintliness, of heroism, of decency, of sportingness, and so on, but this would give to their theory still more the appearance of utilizing the advantages of theft over honest toil.

Thus as moral theorists we need to discover some theory that will allow for both absolute duties, which, in Mill's phrase, can be exacted from a man like a debt, to omit which is to do wrong and to deserve censure, and which may be embodied in formal rules or principles, and also for a range of actions which are of moral value and which an agent may feel called upon to perform, but which cannot be demanded and whose omission cannot be called wrongdoing. Traditional moral theories, I have suggested, fail to do this. It would be well beyond the scope of this paper, and probably beyond my capacity, to produce here and now a full moral theory designed to accommodate all these facts, including the facts of saintliness and heroism. But I do think that of all traditional theories utilitarianism can be most easily modified to accommodate the facts, and would like before ending this paper to bring forward some considerations tending to support this point of view.

Moore went to great pains to determine exactly the nature of the intrinsically good, and Mill to discover the *summum bonum*, Moore's aim being to explain thereby directly the rightness and wrongness of particular actions and Mill's to justify a set of moral principles in the light of which the rightness or wrongness of particular actions can be decided. But, though there can be very tricky problems of duty, they do not naturally present themselves as problems whose solution depends upon an exact determination of an ultimate end; while the moral principles that come most readily to mind—truth-telling; promise-keeping; abstinence from murder, theft, and violence; and the like—make a nice discrimination of the supreme good seem irrelevant. We do not need to debate whether it is Moore's string of intrinsic goods or Mill's happiness that is achieved by conformity to such principles; it is enough to see that without them social life would be impossible and any life would indeed be solitary, poor, nasty, brutish, and short. Even self-interest (which some have seen as the sole foundation of morality) is sufficient ground to render it wise to preach, if not to practice, such principles. Such considerations as these, which are not novel, have led some utilitarians to treat avoidance of the *summum malum* rather than the achievement of the *summum bonum* as the foundation of morality. Yet to others this has seemed, with some justification, to assign to morality too ignoble a place.

But the facts we have been considering earlier in this paper are surely relevant at this point. It is absurd to ask just what ideal is being served by abstinence from murder; but on the other hand nobody could see in acts of heroism such as we have been considering a mere avoidance of antisocial behavior. Here we have something more gracious, actions that need to be inspired by a positive ideal. If duty can, as Mill said, be exacted from persons as a debt, it is because duty is a minimum requirement for living together; the positive contribution of actions that go beyond duty could not be so exacted.

It may, however, be objected that this is a glorification of the higher flights of morality at the expense of duty, toward which an unduly cynical attitude is being taken. In so far as the suggestion is that we are forgetting how hard the way of duty may be and that doing one's duty can at times deserve to be called heroic and saintly, the answer is that we have mentioned this and acknowledge it; it is not forgotten but irrelevant to the point at issue, which is the place of duty in a moral classification of actions, not the problem of the worth of moral agents. But I may be taken to be acquiescing in a low and circumscribed view of duty which I may be advised to enlarge. We should, it may be said, hitch our wagons to the stars and not be content to say: you must do this and that as duties, and it would be very nice if you were to do these other things but we do not expect them of you. Is it perhaps only an imperfect conception of duty which finds it not to comprise the whole of morality? I want to examine this difficulty quite frankly, and to explain why I think that we properly recognize morality that goes beyond duty; for it seems to me incontestable that properly or improperly we do so.

No intelligent person will claim infallibility for his moral views. But allowing for this one must claim that one's moral code is ideal so far as one can see; for to say, "I recognize moral code A but see clearly that moral code B is superior to it," is but a way of saying that one recognizes moral code B but is only prepared to live up to moral code A. In some sense, then, everybody must be prepared to justify his moral code as ideal; but some philosophers have misunderstood this sense. Many philosophers have thought it necessary, if they were to defend their moral code as ideal, to try to show that it had a superhuman, a priori validity. Kant, for example, tried to show that the moral principles he accepted were such as any rational being, whether man or angel, must inevitably accept; the reputedly empiricist Locke thought that it must be possible to work out a deductive justification of moral laws. In making such claims such philosophers have unintentionally done morality a disservice; for their failure to show that the moral code was ideal in the sense of being a rationally justifiable system independent of time, place, circumstance, and human nature has led many to conclude that there can be no justification of a moral code, that moral codes are a matter of taste or convention.

But morality, I take it, is something that should serve human needs, not something that incidentally sweeps man up with itself, and to show that a morality was ideal would be to show that it best served man—man as he is and as he can be expected to become, not man as he would be if he were perfectly rational or an incorporeal angel. Just as it would be fatuous to build our machines so that they would give the best results according to an abstract conception of mechanical principles, and is much more desirable to design them to withstand to some extent our ham-fistedness, ignorance, and carelessness, so our morality must be one that will work. In the only sense of "ideal" that is of importance in action, it is part of the ideal that a moral code should actually help to contribute to human well-being, and a moral code that would work only for angels (for whom it would in any case be unnecessary) would be a far from ideal moral code for human beings. There is, indeed, a place for ideals that are practically unworkable in human affairs, as there is a place for the blueprint of a machine that will never go into production; but it is not the place of such ideals to serve as a basic code of duties.

If, then, we are aiming at a moral code that will best serve human needs, a code that is ideal in the sense that a world in which such a code is acknowledged will be a better place than a world in which some other sort of moral code is acknowledged, it seems that there are ample grounds why our code should distinguish between basic rules, summarily set forth in simple rules and binding on all, and the higher flights of morality of which saintliness and heroism are outstanding examples. These grounds I shall enumerate at once.

1. It is important to give a special status of urgency, and to exert exceptional pressure, in those matters in which compliance with the demands of morality by all is indispensable. An army without men of heroic valor would be impoverished, but without general attention to the duties laid down in military law it would become a mere rabble. Similarly, while life in a world without its saints and heroes would be impoverished, it would only be poor and not necessarily brutish or short as when basic duties are neglected.

2. If we are to exact basic duties like debts, and censure failure, such duties must be, in ordinary circumstances, within the capacity of the ordinary man. It would be silly for us to say to ourselves, our children and our fellow men, "This and

that you and everyone else must do," if the acts in question are such that manifestly but few could bring themselves to do them, though we may ourselves resolve to try to be of that few. To take a parallel from positive law, the prohibition laws asked too much of the American people and were consequently broken systematically; and as people got used to breaking the law a general lowering of respect for the law naturally followed; it no longer seemed that a law was something that everybody could be expected to obey. Similarly in Britain the gambling laws, some of which are utterly unpractical, have fallen into contempt as a body. So, if we were to represent the heroic act of sacrificing one's life for one's comrades as a basic duty, the effect would be to lower the degree of urgency and stringency that the notion of duty does in fact possess. The basic moral code must not be in part too far beyond the capacity of the ordinary men on ordinary occasions, or a general breakdown of compliance with the moral code would be an inevitable consequence; duty would seem to be something high and unattainable, and not for "the likes of us." Admirers of the Sermon on the Mount do not in practice, and could not, treat failure to turn the other cheek and to give one's cloak also as being on all fours with breaches of the Ten Commandments, however earnestly they themselves try to live a Christian life.

3. A moral code, if it is to be a code, must be formulable, and if it is to be a code to be observed it must be formulable in rules of manageable complexity. The ordinary man has to apply and interpret this code without recourse to a Supreme Court or House of Lords. But one can have such rules only in cases in which a type of action that is reasonably easy to recognize is almost invariably desirable or undesirable, as killing is almost invariably undesirable and promise-keeping almost invariably desirable. Where no definite rule of manageable complexity can be justified, we cannot work on that moral plane on which types of action can be enjoined or condemned

as duty or crime. It has no doubt often been the case that a person who has gone off to distant parts to nurse lepers has thereby done a deed of great moral worth. But such an action is not merely too far beyond average human capacity to be regarded as a duty, as was insisted in (2) above; it would be quite ridiculous for everyone, however circumstanced, to be expected to go off and nurse lepers. But it would be absurd to try to formulate complicated rules to determine in just what circumstances such an action is a duty. This same point can readily be applied to such less spectacular matters as excusing legitimate debts or nursing sick neighbors.

4. It is part of the notion of a duty that we have a right to demand compliance from others even when we are interested parties. I may demand that you keep your promises to me, tell me the truth, and do me no violence, and I may reproach you if you transgress. But however admirable the tending of strangers in sickness may be it is not a basic duty, and we are not entitled to reproach those to whom we are strangers if they do not tend us in sickness; nor can I tell you, if you fail to give me a cigarette when I have run out, that you have failed in your duty to me, however much you may subsequently reproach yourself for your meanness if you do so fail. A line must be drawn between what we can expect and demand from others and what we can merely hope for and receive with gratitude when we get it; duty falls on one side of this line, and other acts with moral value on the other, and rightly so.

5. In the case of basic moral duties we act to some extent under constraint. We have no choice but to apply pressure on each other to conform in these fundamental matters; here moral principles are like public laws rather than like private ideals. But free choice of the better course of action is always preferable to action under pressure, even when the pressure is but moral. When possible, therefore, it is better that pressure should not be applied and that there should be encour-

agement and commendation for performance rather than outright demands and censure in the event of nonperformance. There are no doubt degrees in this matter. Some pressure may reasonably be brought to persuade a person to go some way beyond basic duty in the direction of kindliness and forbearance, to be not merely a just man but also not too hard a man. But, while there is nothing whatever objectionable in the idea of someone's being pressed to carry out such a basic duty as promise-keeping, there is something horrifying in the thought of pressure being brought on him to perform an act of heroism. Though the man might feel himself morally called upon to do the deed, it would be a moral outrage to apply pressure on him to do such a deed as sacrificing his life for others.

These five points make it clear why I do not think that the distinction of basic duty from other acts of moral worth, which I claim to detect in ordinary moral thought, is a sign of the inferiority of our everyday moral thinking to that of the general run of moral theorists. It in no way involves anyone in acquiescing in a second best. No doubt from the agent's point of view it is imperative that he should endeavor to live up to the highest ideals of behavior that he can think of, and if an action falls within the ideal it is for him irrelevant whether or not it is a duty or some more supererogatory act. But it simply does not follow that the distinction is in every way unimportant, for it is important that we should not demand ideal conduct from others in the way in which we must demand basic morality from them, or blame them equally for failures in all fields. It is not cynicism to make the minimum positive demands upon one's fellow men; but to characterize an act as a duty is so to demand it.

Thus we may regard the imperatives of duty as prohibiting behavior that is intolerable if men are to live together in society and demanding the minimum of cooperation toward the same end; that is why we have to treat compliance as compulsory and dereliction as liable to public censure. We do not need to ask with Bentham whether pushpin is as good as poetry, with Mill whether it is better to be Socrates dissatisfied or a fool satisfied, or with Moore whether a beautiful world with no one to see it would have intrinsic worth; what is and what is not tolerable in society depends on no such nice discrimination. Utilitarians, when attempting to justify the main rules of duty in terms of a *summum bonum*, have surely invoked many different types of utilitarian justification, ranging from the avoidance of the intolerable to the fulfillment of the last detail of a most rarefied ideal.

Thus I wish to suggest that utilitarianism can best accommodate the facts to which I have drawn attention; but I have not wished to support any particular view about the supreme good or the importance of pleasure. By utilitarianism I mean only a theory that moral justification of actions must be in terms of results. We can be content to say that duty is mainly concerned with the avoidance of intolerable results, while other forms of moral behavior have more positive aims.

To summarize, I have suggested that the trichotomy of duties, indifferent actions, and wrongdoing is inadequate. There are many kinds of action that involve going beyond duty proper, saintly and heroic actions being conspicuous examples of such kinds of action. It has been my main concern to note this point and to ask moral philosophers to theorize in a way that does not tacitly deny it, as most traditional theories have. But I have also been so rash as to suggest that we may look upon our duties as basic requirements to be universally demanded as providing the only tolerable basis of social life. The higher flights of morality can then be regarded as more positive contributions that go beyond what is universally to be exacted; but while not exacted publicly they are clearly equally pressing *in foro interno* on those who are not content merely to avoid the intolerable. Whether this should be called a version of utilitarianism, as I suggest, is a matter of small moment.